THE HUMAN HORIZON

A Field Guide to Staying Human in an Age of Extremes

Lee Scott

Original Edition — Mar 2026

Original Edition ISBNs: Trade Paperback 979-8-9954713-2-5; EPUB 979-8-9954713-3-2.

www.leescottbooks.com

Cover art concept by the Author.

Graphic design/layout by TheArtBoxOnline@gmail.com

Table of Contents

Author's Note   IX
A Reader's Challenge

Transparency Tally   XIII

Preface   XVI

Epigraph   XXI
  Feet on the Ground
  Eyes Forward
  Stay Human

Part 1   1
Seeing Clearly

1. The Horizon Is Where Humans Live   2
    Why Orientation to Reality Precedes Judgment

2. Orientation Comes Before Belief   9
    Why Perception Determines What You Think Is True

3. The Two Escapes   15
    Why Humans Drift Toward Illusion When Reality Is
    Costly

4. The Care and Corruption of Lenses   21
    How Perception Filters Reality Before Judgment

Part 2   25
The Disciplines That Stabilize Reality

5. The Discipline of Proportion   26
    Why Stability Requires Restraint in an Age of Ex-
    tremes

6. Literacy and Shared Reality   32
    Why Reading Is the Infrastructure of Civilization

7. Competence Grounds Responsibility   37
    Why Capability Precedes Authority

8. Humility Preserves Learning   43
    Why Intellectual Humility Protects Reality

9. Words Mean Things   47
    Why Language Collapse Precedes Civilizational Col-
    lapse

Part 3   52
The Structures That Sustain Civilization

10. Civilization Is a Relay Race   53
    Why Each Generation Maintains What It Did Not
    Build

11. Obligation Does Not End With You   57
    Why Responsibility Extends Across Generations

12. Conflict Must Be Contained, Not Eliminated   62
    Why Civilization Requires Managed Tension

13. Repair Is Not Romantic   67
    Why Maintenance Sustains What Ideals Alone Cannot

14. Scale Demands Governance, Not Moral Shortcuts   72
    Why Large Systems Require Structure

15. Governance Is Not Salvation   80
    Why Institutions Stabilize Power but Do Not Redeem It

Part 4   86
The Human Mechanism

16. Living at the Horizon   87
    Why Orientation Restores Proportion, Meaning, and Endurance

17. Human Override   93
    The Gap Between Stimulus and Response

18. Maintenance is Not a Hymn   102
    Why Civilization Endures Through Structure, Not Faith

19. Ego Under Pressure   109
    Where Override Is Most Likely to Fail

Part 5   122
The Retun to Human Scale

20. The Collapse of Scale   123
    Why Systems Fail When Growth Outpaces Governance

21. The Anti-Human Horizon   133
    Balance Requires Correction

22. Skepticism vs Cynicism   141
    Why Doubt Can Clarify Reality or Destroy It

23. Village, Not Tribe   149
    Why Civilization Requires Reintegration

24. Final Orientation   160
    How Humans Remain Aligned in an Unstable World

25. Afterword   169

Dedications

This book is personally dedicated to:

My Mother, the quiet force behind everything I am.

My Father, who chose love when it mattered most.

My Step-Parents, for the steady presence that shaped me.

My biological Father, never known and now gone; peace in the unknown, for us both.

My beloved Grandparents, whose lives still echo in mine.

My close and far friends, a network as varied as life itself, yet bound by an unmistakable common thread that still humbles me.

My Nephews, may you build wisely.

My Brothers, especially BB, who bore the weight of an often unkind world, protected me, and carried that burden with strength and dignity until the end.

My three amazing Daughters, whose impact is immeasurable and whose light defines my world.

And to the woman who stands beside me—steady, calm, and truly kind. Her quiet strength means more than words can say.

This book is also dedicated to the keepers of the horizon:

To the clergy who choose reform over rigidity.
To the workers who build, maintain, and repair civilization.
To the scientists and medical community who carry the burden
when imbalance turns into harm.
To the artists who remind us what humanity is for.
And to the ordinary people who choose restraint, responsibility,
and human dignity over tribal impulse.
When humanity is good, it is astonishing.
This book is for those who keep that possibility alive.

Author's Note

A Reader's Challenge

THIS BOOK DOES NOT argue for a worldview. It describes observable mechanisms—patterns of behavior, coordination, responsibility, and failure that recur across individuals, institutions, and societies regardless of ideology.

The claims in this book were not constructed from theory and then applied outward. They were assembled from repeated observation: how people behave under pressure, how systems drift when responsibility diffuses, how coordination falters when incentives misalign, and how collapse often appears ordinary long before it becomes unavoidable.

This book does not ask you to adopt a moral identity. It does not ask you to signal virtue. It does not ask you to agree. Its claims are narrower than that. Each chapter isolates a specific mechanism, names it plainly, and describes how it tends to operate within defined boundaries. Where possible, claims are framed so they can be challenged directly rather than absorbed emotionally. Description precedes prescription. Precision precedes opinion.

If you are looking for motivation, ideology, or reassurance, this book will likely disappoint you. If you are willing to locate claims, examine them, and reject them cleanly where you believe they fail, this book will meet you there.

You do not owe me agreement. You owe yourself intellectual clarity.

I did not learn this orientation from ideology or formal schooling; I learned it from honest, calm people encountered in daily life—the steady back and forth of human statements and human reactions, the quiet corrections that come from living among others, and the long accumulation of consequences that follow both wisdom and error.

Some of those influences were real individuals who modeled proportion, restraint, and clarity. Others were cultural teachers—figures such as Mister Rogers and Mister Spock—whose plain speech and disciplined reasoning shaped an entire generation's understanding of responsibility, civility, and truth.

Much of it came from the broader book of life itself: a path marked by sharp reversals, unexpected turns, moments of life-threatening violence, and periods of rebuilding that followed. It was a life shaped by the discovery that much of what I believed about my own history was untrue, and that the truth—when it finally surfaced later in life—was far more difficult than the story that preceded it.

That revelation would have broken many people. Yet, even without full honesty, my mother chose to prepare me in another way. She strengthened discipline, resilience, and endurance long before the reasons for those qualities became clear. When the truth arrived, those foundations held.

The perspective in this book was not formed in comfort or theory. It was formed under pressure, through repeated exposure to consequence, recovery, and responsibility. If these observations help even one person navigate hardship with greater clarity or steadiness, the purpose of sharing them is fulfilled.

A Reader's Challenge

The claims in this book are meant to describe observable mechanisms. You are invited to challenge any of them. If you believe a claim does not hold weight, ask:

What specific statement do I believe is false?

What evidence contradicts it?

What alternative explanation better accounts for the same outcomes?

Disagreement is not a failure of reading. Vagueness is.

This book does not ask you to agree. It asks you to think precisely and respond honestly.

TRANSPARENCY TALLY

Author Transparency for an AI World

Transparency Summary

This book was conceived, directed, and written by a human author. AI-assisted editorial tools were used to organize material, refine language, challenge clarity, identify gaps, and support consistency. They were not used to invent the book, originate the core message, or replace the author's judgment. The author generated the concepts, defined revisions, set tone and direction, and approved all final language.

Radar is the working name of the custom AI-assisted editorial agent configured by the author for this project. Radar is not a company, commercial product, outside editor, or outside service.

Transparency Tally

Primary Author / Core Concepts — Lee Scott — **86%**

Editorial / Structuring Support — AI-assisted editor — **12%**

Core Concept Refinement — AI-assisted editor — **2%**

Total — 100% Clear

Transparency Tally Concept

The Transparency Tally is a public-use authorship transparency disclosure standard created by Lee Scott. This term is intentionally released for open free use so that anyone may apply it. No person or entity may claim exclusive ownership of the name.

This standard was developed out of necessity and principle in the modern era of collaborative writing tools. Its purpose is to make authorship visible, understandable, and accountable when artificial intelligence or other support tools are used to assist creative work.

Much of the work behind this book was produced in a semi-independent environment where resources were limited and hiring assistants was not financially possible. Writing had to be done alone, often without institutional support or editorial staff. At the same time, there was growing concern about a modern practice in publishing and online content: individuals presenting work under their own name that they did not meaningfully write.

That conflict created a clear need for structure. Rather than reject technology, the author established a disciplined process around it.

A custom AI-assisted editorial agent, internally named Radar, was used as a working scribe, structure checker, clarity challenger, and consistency tool. Radar helped organize dictated material, test whether sections remained clear, identify repetition or drift, refine structure, and return editorial decisions to the author.

Radar was not used as a ghostwriter. Radar did not originate the book's thesis, moral framework, chapter architecture, field observations, lived experience, judgments, or final language authority. The author remained responsible for the ideas, structure, tone, revisions, and final approval of all language.

This arrangement is no different in principle from an author working with a traditional publishing team of editors and assistants, except that the author retained more direct control over content, voice, and final decisions than is typically granted under standard book publishing agreements.

The reference scale provides a consistent method for documenting contributions from both human and AI-assisted collaborators.

Reference Scale — Authorship Contribution

Proofreader or Typist — 0–5%

Editor or Scribe — 10–35%

Developmental Editor — 25–40%

Ghostwriter — 35–95%

Primary Author — 60–95%

PEOPLE KEEP CHOOSING EXTREMES. Some live with their eyes buried in the dirt. Others live with their eyes fixed on the sky. Both believe they are seeing clearly. Both are escaping.

The person staring at the ground calls themselves grounded, practical, hardened by reality. They speak of grit and survival, of endurance and toughness, as though nothing matters beyond what is directly in front of them. Persistence becomes virtue. Isolation becomes strength. But this story omits the systems, inheritances, and relationships that made survival possible in the first place. It converts dependence into denial.

The person staring at the sky calls themselves awake, enlightened, attuned to something higher. At times the language becomes absolute, as though ultimate meaning has already been secured. This is where distortion enters. Complete certainty about ultimate causation is not available while alive. That limitation is not an attack on faith. It is what preserves faith as faith rather than collapsing it into proof.

Human perception is narrow by design. We live from field level, not from the skybox. Our horizon is local. Even our greatest instruments—telescopes, equations, satellites—extend inference, not omniscience. We can measure distance and composition. We can detect patterns and model trajectories. But meaning, purpose, and final causation remain beyond direct verification. When certainty outruns evidence, fiction quietly replaces humility.

The error is not acknowledging that something lies beyond us. The error is pretending we possess it fully. Orientation fails not when people admit mystery, but when they deny their limits.

This book is not about choosing between those camps. It is about refusing both. There is only one sustainable place for human life: not below the horizon, not above it, but within it.

The horizon is not compromise. It is not dilution. It is a functional operating plane—physical, psychological, and moral. The ground remains beneath us. The sky remains above us. But life unfolds in the middle, where consequence meets aspiration, where reality meets responsibility, and where meaning must coexist with limitation.

Feet on the ground. Eyes forward. This is not poetry. It is anatomy.

When humans lose this orientation, the damage is rarely dramatic at first. Judgment blurs. Proportion erodes. Language inflates. Fantasy and grievance replace responsibility. Some escape downward into resentment and survivalism, shrinking their world until endurance becomes identity. Others escape upward into rescue myths and moral spectacle, dissolving responsibility into slogans, visions, or promised deliverance. Both feel convincing from the inside. Both become destructive over time.

The horizon posture is uncomfortable because it removes escape routes. It accepts reality without surrendering meaning. It accepts limits without abandoning aspiration. It accepts responsibility without dramatizing despair. It offers no spectacle and no guarantee of triumph. It offers coherence.

This book attempts to name that posture clearly, defend it against distortion, and describe what it looks like—personally, culturally, and civically—to live there. Not perfectly. Not heroically. But honestly.

This book is not a weapon. It is a lens. If it is used to narrow moral concern, justify tribal hostility, or elevate dominance, it has been misread. The purpose of this framework is to preserve proportion and shared reality, not fracture them. The lens described here restores dimensionality; it does not collapse it into advantage.

These observations were shaped between the California coast and the red clay of Oklahoma—between coastal mesas, high deserts, mountains, and working fields—where scale and consequence are lived rather than theorized.

Feet on the Ground

Eyes Forward

Stay Human

PART 1

Seeing Clearly

THE HORIZON IS WHERE HUMANS LIVE

Why Orientation to Reality Precedes Judgment

ORIENTATION PRECEDES EVALUATION IN all functional systems. In plain terms, you cannot judge what is happening if you are not accurately positioned to see it. Identity may anchor beliefs, but identity is not itself a belief about conditions. Calling yourself something does not establish anything about reality. Judgment depends on accurate contact with conditions as they exist, rather than as they are preferred, feared, or imagined.

This is not a minor error when it fails. Entire careers collapse because someone misread conditions. Institutions fracture because leaders misjudged scale or timing. Relationships deteriorate because perception hardened before understanding occurred. History is filled with decisions that felt coherent to those making them but were detached from the circumstances they claimed to address.

When orientation is incomplete or distorted, conclusions may appear internally consistent while remaining externally false. A system can generate disciplined reasoning and still move confidently in the wrong direction. This chapter examines the mechanism by which orientation enables or disables judgment.

In this sense, orientation functions like equilibrium: an internal balance extended outward into perception and action. Without equilibrium, movement continues, but coordination fails. Effort increases. Confidence may increase. But alignment quietly disappears.

The mechanism described here applies to situations in which judgment depends on external conditions that exist independently of the observer's beliefs or intentions. It governs domains such as physical environments, shared social systems, material constraints, and factual states that can be misperceived, ignored, exaggerated, or denied. It does not apply to purely internal preferences, aesthetic tastes, or value choices that do not claim correspondence with external reality. The mechanism concerns contact with conditions, not agreement about meaning.

Where no external condition is being assessed, orientation does not function as a prerequisite in the same way. The claim here is deliberately limited: where judgment depends on shared or external conditions, orientation is a prerequisite; where it does not, the mechanism does not apply. The boundary matters because overextension would weaken the claim. Orientation governs contact with reality, not personal taste.

Orientation is often confused with intelligence, expertise, or moral seriousness. These are adjacent but distinct capacities. Intelligence may accelerate reasoning without correcting faulty inputs. Expertise may deepen interpretation while leaving foundational misalignment untouched. Moral seriousness may intensify judgment while amplifying error if orientation is absent. Orientation is neither reasoning nor evaluation; it is the act of accurately situating oneself relative to conditions. Judgment begins only after this positioning occurs, regardless of the observer's cognitive speed or ethical intensity.

When orientation erodes, judgment does not cease; it reorganizes around substitutes. Assumptions replace observation. Narratives fill gaps left by missing contact. Confidence may increase even as accuracy declines, because internal coherence is mistaken for external alignment. In this state, disagreement appears as hostility rather than an informational discrepancy, and correction is experienced as threat rather than refinement. The system remains active but self-referential, generating judgments that circulate internally without recalibration against conditions.

Humans are upright creatures. That fact is so ordinary it nearly disappears from notice, yet it explains more about our failures, personal and collective, than many complicated theories. We are not built to crawl. We are not built to float. We are not built to live with our faces permanently tilted upward or downward. Our physical design implies a natural posture.

Orientation is not only vertical. Humans can lose alignment laterally as well, becoming fixed to one side or another. But this book is not concerned with left or right. Lateral fixation is a downstream effect, not a primary failure. When vertical orientation collapses, when people lose contact with ground or horizon, lateral identity hardens automatically. The problem is not which side someone stands on, but that they are no longer standing upright in relation to reality.

This book addresses the conditions that precede division, not the divisions that follow from it. Our balance depends on a level visual plane. Our coordination depends on forward orientation. Our survival depends on seeing what is coming, not only what is beneath our feet or permanently out of reach.

The ground is always beneath us. The sky is always above us. But life is not lived in either extreme. Life is lived along the horizon line, the forward plane where reality, consequence, responsibility, and choice intersect. This is not metaphorical in the decorative sense. It is biological and functional. Force a person to walk while staring straight down and they will slow, stumble, and eventually fall. Force them to walk while staring straight up and they will drift, collide, and lose orientation.

Functional movement requires forward vision. The horizon is not optional. When people lose this orientation, they do not merely lose perspective; they lose judgment. The horizon is not an idea layered on top of human life. It is the operating plane that makes coordinated human life possible at all.

Feet planted. Eyes forward. That is the posture.

When humans abandon this posture, thinking collapses into distortion. Some collapse downward into fixation on survival, grievance, scarcity, and threat. Others collapse upward into abstraction, fantasy, ideology, moral certainty, or rescue myths. Both postures feel convincing from the inside. Both feel justified. Both claim insight. Both fail over time because they detach from full contact with conditions.

A downward-oriented person experiences the world primarily as pressure. Everything feels scarce. Time feels short.

Every interaction feels competitive. Responsibility narrows into self-protection. The future shrinks until it barely exists beyond immediate survival.

An upward-oriented person experiences the world primarily as concept. Consequences feel distant or adjustable. Responsibility feels transferable. Reality becomes something that should eventually yield to belief, intention, or insistence. The present becomes thin, provisional, almost inconvenient.

Neither posture begins as insanity. Both begin as protection. Looking down keeps you from falling. Looking up helps you navigate beyond immediate obstacles. The failure begins when posture hardens into identity and becomes exclusive. Once orientation freezes, belief rushes in to defend it. Convictions form not to discover truth, but to justify position. Evidence is filtered. Language bends. Responsibility is reassigned. Reality becomes negotiable.

The horizon posture interrupts this collapse. It does not deny danger, nor does it deny aspiration. It accepts gravity without surrendering meaning. It accepts limits without abandoning hope. It accepts responsibility without dramatizing despair. It allows tension without demanding escape.

This is why the horizon feels demanding. It offers no exit into simplification. It does not let you hide in nostalgia or fantasy. It does not let you outsource adulthood to systems, saviors, or abstractions. It asks you to stand where you are, see what is coming, and act accordingly.

This posture is often mistaken for compromise or weakness. It is neither. The horizon is not the midpoint between extremes.

It is the rejection of extremes as governing postures. It is functional maturity.

At their best, our strongest human systems operate here. Science, at its best, does not invent explanations that violate observable reality. It advances cautiously, revising belief in response to evidence rather than desire. Tradition, at its best, preserves what works without romanticizing the past. It carries knowledge forward without assuming earlier eras were purer or wiser by default. Faith, at its best, inspires humility rather than exemption. It motivates responsibility rather than escape. It acknowledges mystery without surrendering coherence.

These systems fail when posture fails. They harden when orientation is lost. What begins as tool becomes identity. What begins as guidance becomes insulation.

A horizon-oriented human understands that life always contains tension, between what is and what could be, between responsibility and desire, between inheritance and innovation. The horizon does not eliminate this tension. It makes it navigable. It prevents tension from collapsing into fragmentation.

When people abandon the horizon, societies fracture. Language decays. Competence erodes. Fantasies replace plans. Grievances replace responsibility. Systems fail not because no one cared, but because too many people were looking only up or only down.

This book begins here because everything else depends on orientation. Before belief. Before ideology. Before judgment. There is posture. If the posture is wrong, nothing built on top of it will hold.

The horizon is where humans live. Everything that follows depends on whether we are willing to stand there consistently.

Chapter 1 Resolve

If you remember nothing else from this chapter, remember this:

Sound judgment depends on maintaining orientation to reality before forming beliefs, positions, or conclusions. Without accurate positioning, even intelligent reasoning will misfire.

What This Chapter Is

A description of orientation as a physical and cognitive posture toward reality

An explanation of how loss of orientation distorts judgment

A distinction between horizon orientation and upward or downward fixation

An account of how stable orientation enables responsibility and coherent action

What This Chapter Is Not

An argument for moderation or compromise between ideologies

A claim that extremes are morally wrong rather than structurally unstable

A statement about which beliefs, values, or identities are correct

ORIENTATION COMES BEFORE BELIEF

Why Perception Determines What You Think Is True

BELIEFS EMERGE AS STABILIZATIONS of interpreted experience. They depend on prior contact with conditions that supply raw constraints. When beliefs precede orientation, they function as filters rather than conclusions. This chapter examines how belief formation follows orientation and how reversal of this order alters system behavior. This mechanism applies to beliefs that claim explanatory or predictive power about the external world. It governs factual, causal, and structural beliefs that purport to describe how things are or will be. It does not govern provisional hypotheses explicitly held as tentative, nor symbolic beliefs that do not assert correspondence with conditions. The mechanism addresses belief as a settled orientation outcome, not as a temporary mental tool used during exploration.

Belief is often conflated with opinion, identity, or commitment. An opinion may change with little consequence and does not necessarily constrain perception. Identity may stabilize belief, but it is not itself a statement about how reality works. Commitment reflects persistence, not accuracy. Belief, in this context, is a stabilized interpretation that resists revision because it has been internalized as orientation.

Confusing belief with preference or loyalty obscures its role in shaping perception before judgment occurs. When beliefs precede orientation, perception reorganizes to defend the belief rather than inform it. Incoming information is sorted by compatibility instead of relevance. Ambiguity is resolved prematurely, and disconfirming signals are treated as noise or threat.

Over time, the belief becomes less about explaining conditions and more about maintaining internal consistency. The system narrows its intake while increasing its certainty, reducing adaptive capacity without an explicit decision to do so.

Most people believe their opinions are formed by reasoning. They imagine a process that looks something like this: they encounter information, evaluate it, decide what is true, and then form beliefs based on evidence. That is not how human beings work.Long before anyone adopts a political position, a religious belief, or a philosophical worldview, they have already decided, usually unconsciously, what kind of world they believe they are living in and what kind of role they believe they occupy within it. That decision comes first. Belief comes later.

Orientation is not a conclusion. It is a filter. It determines what feels relevant, what feels threatening, what feels dismissible, and what feels morally urgent before conscious thought ever begins. By the time someone is articulating beliefs, their orientation has already shaped what evidence they noticed, how they interpreted it, and which explanations felt plausible. This is why people can look at the same facts and come away convinced of entirely opposite truths, not because one side is intelligent and the other is not, but because the information passed through different internal filters before it was ever evaluated.

Orientation quietly answers a set of questions most people never realize they are asking: Is the world fundamentally hostile or manageable? Is responsibility primarily personal or external? Are outcomes mostly shaped by effort, by systems, or by fate? Is the future something to prepare for, resist, or wait out?

Once these questions are answered, implicitly, emotionally, and often early in life, belief systems assemble themselves around the answers. This is why arguing ideology rarely works. Belief feels primary because it is visible. Orientation is quieter because it operates beneath language. Before a person declares what they think, they have already decided how they are positioned.

Orientation determines what information feels threatening, what feels affirming, and what feels irrelevant. It sets the emotional baseline from which belief is constructed. Orientation answers a more primitive question than belief does. Belief asks, "What is true?" Orientation asks, "Where am I standing?" If the stance is defensive, belief will select defensively. If the stance is resentful, belief will organize around grievance. If the stance is curious, belief remains provisional and revisable. This is why arguments rarely change people. Arguments target belief. Orientation determines whether those arguments are even permitted to land. In simple terms, before you decide what you think, you have already decided how you are standing.

Orientation is often mistaken for personality or temperament, but it is a cultivated posture. It can harden through repeated exposure to outrage, humiliation, or fear. It can also strengthen through literacy, humility, and proportionality. Because orientation shapes interpretation, it becomes self-reinforcing. A hostile stance produces hostile readings of events, which then confirm the stance.

In simple terms, the stance you take today shapes the world you see tomorrow. When people debate beliefs, they are usually trying to modify the output without touching the filter that produced it. Evidence is presented. Logic is sharpened. Counterexamples are offered. And nothing moves, not because the argument is weak, but because it never reaches the level where the real decision was made.

Orientation determines what counts as evidence in the first place. A person who experiences the world primarily as something happening to them will gravitate toward explanations that emphasize external forces, manipulation, or betrayal. Responsibility will feel suspect. Success will feel unfair. Failure will feel imposed. A person who experiences the world primarily as something unfolding above them will gravitate toward explanations that emphasize inevitability, destiny, or historical correction. Responsibility will feel abstract. Present consequences will feel provisional. Outcomes will feel prewritten.

Neither of these orientations require conscious intent. They emerge naturally from experience, temperament, and reinforcement. But once established, they strongly constrain which belief systems feel obvious, reasonable, or unavoidable. Ideology then performs a stabilizing function. It provides language that makes an orientation feel principled rather than reactive. It supplies narratives that justify why responsibility should be resisted, deferred, or displaced. It offers certainty, identity, and community, all without requiring the person to revisit the underlying orientation that produced it.

This is why ideology so often becomes identity. Once belief is fused to self-concept, evidence no longer functions as information. It functions as a threat. Challenges are not evaluated; they are deflected. Questions are not explored; they are interpreted as attacks. At that point, debate is no longer about truth. It is about protection.

This chapter matters because it explains why so many modern conversations feel circular, hostile, and unproductive. People are not failing to reason. They are reasoning after orientation has already done the decisive work. Changing belief without addressing orientation is like repainting a structure with a cracked foundation. The surface changes, but failures persist. The goal is not to eliminate belief. Humans require frameworks of meaning. The goal is to recognize the order in which things really happen, to understand that orientation shapes perception, perception shapes belief, and belief shapes action.

If that order is ignored, nothing built on top of it will hold. The next chapter names the two most common ways people avoid confronting this problem altogether. They do not argue about orientation. They flee from it.

Chapter 2 Resolve

If you remember nothing else from this chapter, remember this:

Belief forms after orientation and functions to stabilize a prior filter rather than determine truth.

What This Chapter Is

An explanation of how orientation precedes conscious belief formation

A description of orientation as a perceptual filter that shapes what counts as evidence

An account of how belief systems assemble around pre-existing orientation

A clarification of why belief becomes defensive once fused to identity

A structural explanation for why ideological debate fails to produce change

What This Chapter Is Not

A claim that any specific belief system is false or illegitimate

An argument for or against responsibility, fate, systems, or effort

A moral judgment about people who hold strong beliefs

THE TWO ESCAPES

Why Humans Drift Toward Illusion When Reality Is Costly

ESCAPE IS OFTEN CONFUSED with rest, abstraction, or strategic delay. Rest suspends engagement to restore capacity without denying conditions. Abstraction simplifies complexity while preserving reference to reality. Delay postpones action while maintaining orientation. Escape differs in that it replaces contact with substitution. Attention shifts from conditions to narratives, identities, or extremes that feel resolving without requiring alignment. The distinction lies in whether the system remains oriented during withdrawal.

When escape mechanisms dominate, they become self-reinforcing. Relief from tension is mistaken for resolution, encouraging repetition. Orientation decays further as substitutes gain emotional or symbolic weight. Over time, escapes harden into patterns that appear purposeful but remain disconnected from constraints. The system expends energy maintaining distance from reality rather than adjusting to it, increasing fragility while preserving the appearance of engagement.

Once orientation is set and belief systems begin assembling around it, most people face a problem they would rather not name. Staying present is work. Remaining accountable to reality requires effort, restraint, and sustained attention. It means accepting limits without outsourcing responsibility. It means living without guarantees. Many people do not reject this consciously; they avoid it. Rather than confront orientation directly, they adopt behaviors that allow them to feel resolved without actually being accountable.

Over time, these behaviors harden into recognizable escape patterns. There are two dominant ones. One waits for rescue, and the other pretends the world can be reduced back to something simpler. They appear across politics, religion, culture, and personal identity. They often oppose each other loudly, yet they serve the same psychological function. Both allow people to exit the present.

The First Escape: Waiting to Be Saved

This escape is built around deferral. Responsibility is pushed outward or upward to institutions, leaders, systems, movements, history, technology, or divine intervention. The specifics change; the structure does not. The core belief is simple: this will be handled elsewhere. Action becomes symbolic rather than practical. Moral energy is spent signaling alignment rather than making changes that carry cost. Failure is tolerated because resolution is always expected to arrive later, delivered by something larger and more powerful than the individual.

This deferral escape feels virtuous because it borrows the language of hope, justice, and inevitability. Passivity is framed as patience. Inaction is reframed as faith. The result is predictable: helplessness. When responsibility is permanently deferred, competence never develops. When outcomes are expected to arrive externally, preparation feels unnecessary. People become fluent in explanation and grievance but brittle in practice. The present is treated as temporary. Consequences are treated as negotiable. Effort is treated as optional. This escape does not require belief in anything supernatural. It appears just as easily in secular systems that promise automatic correction, economic, political, or technological. The mechanism is the same: wait, align, trust the process. The cost is always paid later.

The Second Escape: Retreating into Simplicity

The second escape moves in the opposite direction. Instead of deferring responsibility upward, it collapses responsibility inward and backward. Complexity is rejected. Systems are distrusted. The modern world is framed as corrupt, artificial, or illegitimate. The fantasy here is not rescue; it is return. People imagine a simpler past or a purer way of living, stripped of institutions, expertise, and interdependence. Difficulty is romanticized. Hardship is reframed as authenticity. Modern protections are quietly retained while being publicly disowned.

This escape feels honest because it speaks the language of toughness and self-reliance. Withdrawal is framed as integrity. Disengagement is treated as wisdom. Yet it produces fragility all the same. Complex systems do not disappear because they are resented. Interdependence does not vanish because it is denied. Rejecting modern structures without understanding them does not produce resilience; it produces vulnerability masked as pride. This escape avoids responsibility by pretending scale does not exist. It treats civilization as optional while continuing to rely on its benefits. It substitutes aesthetic hardship for real competence.

Why These Escapes Persist

Both escapes succeed because they relieve tension. There is a reason this pressure feels unbearable in a way that ordinary hardship does not. Whether one believes humans emerged through evolution or were deliberately designed, we are built for endurance under constraint, for effort that is bounded, proportional, and resolvable. Our bodies can sustain long exertion when there is feedback: distance covered, ground gained, fatigue felt, relief earned. Walking, working, carrying, repairing, these loads exhaust the body but settle the nervous system because they move toward completion.

The exhaustion many people experience now is different. It is not the fatigue of effort but the fatigue of vigilance without resolution. Attention is held open indefinitely. Responsibility is implied without agency. Conflict is encountered without containment. Abstraction multiplies faster than action can answer it. The body treats this as threat rather than work. Under these conditions, escape is not a moral failure. It is a pressure response. When effort no longer has edges, when strain no longer converts into progress, the system seeks relief wherever it can find it, upward into deferral or downward into simplification. The problem is not that people are unwilling to endure. It is that they are asked to endure without proportion, feedback, or end.

The first escape relieves the tension of responsibility by postponing it. The second relieves the tension of complexity by rejecting it. Neither requires a person to remain oriented in the present, where tradeoffs must be made, costs must be borne, and outcomes are uncertain. Both provide emotional resolution without practical accountability. Because they point in opposite directions, they often mistake each other for enemies rather than mirrors. One accuses the other of laziness. The other accuses the first of delusion. Both avoid the same task: living here, acting now, and accepting responsibility without guarantees.

The deeper problem is not that these escapes are tempting. The problem is that they become identities. Once someone organizes their self-concept around an escape, questioning it feels like an attack. Evidence is filtered. Costs are minimized. Contradictions are justified. The escape becomes permanent. This is where societies stall, not because people disagree, which is normal, but because too many choose exits over engagement. When exits become habitual, presence thins. When presence thins, systems hollow. What remains may look functional, but it cannot carry weight.

Chapter 3 Resolve

If you remember nothing else from this chapter, remember this:

Avoiding orientation produces two dominant escape patterns that remove people from present accountability while preserving emotional resolution.

What This Chapter Is

A structural description of how people avoid sustained presence after orientation is set.

An explanation of two dominant escape mechanisms: upward deferral and downward retreat.

A scope-limited analysis of behavioral patterns across personal, cultural, and institutional contexts.

An account of how repeated escape hardens into identity and weakens practical competence.

What This Chapter Is Not

An argument for or against any political, religious, or cultural group.

A claim that escape is immoral, ignorant, or malicious.

A defense of modern systems or a rejection of tradition.

The Care and Corruption of Lenses

How Perception Filters Reality Before Judgment

A LENS DOES NOT remain clear simply because it once was. Clarity degrades through repetition, comfort, and neglect. It erodes gradually as familiarity replaces scrutiny and belonging replaces examination. The degradation is rarely dramatic. It accumulates quietly through unchallenged assumptions, repeated narratives, and emotional reinforcement. Over time, distortion can feel identical to truth because the curvature has become invisible. Preservation is not an event. It is maintenance.

Emotional contagion leaves residue. Certainty hardens flexibility. Comfort reduces curiosity. When the village becomes a tribe, alignment begins to replace proportion. The tribe narrows moral concern and tightens interpretive boundaries. What begins as cohesion can become enclosure. When enclosure forms, lenses stop adjusting, and once they stop adjusting, distortion no longer feels like distortion. It feels normal.

Kindness functions as a stabilizing discipline within this maintenance process. It widens attention before reaction hardens. It interrupts caricature before distortion becomes identity. It slows interpretation long enough to restore dimensionality.

Kindness is not softness. It is corrective restraint. Without it, even intelligent people can lose proportion while believing they are defending it, because speed, certainty, and indignation can all mimic moral clarity while quietly reducing it.

Not all lenses are built by the people who wear them. Some arrive pre-focused. A pre-focused lens comes with its angle already set. That means you are being told what matters before you have had the chance to decide for yourself. It defines relevance before observation. It assigns hierarchy before evaluation. It frames threat before inquiry. Its appeal lies in efficiency. It reduces cognitive effort and supplies immediate coherence. The world becomes legible quickly. The cost of that efficiency is contraction.

A pre-focused lens selects emphasis in advance. It curates information and repeats emphasis until curvature disappears from awareness. The wearer does not feel manipulated. They feel oriented. The lens provides relief from ambiguity and reduces interpretive labor. When repeated across groups, pre-focused lenses align perception and consolidate narrative stability. Alignment feels like clarity. It can also become a form of control, especially when people begin mistaking shared emphasis for independent judgment.

The distinction between a self-built lens and a handed lens is not intelligence but construction. A self-built lens evolves through friction. It tolerates doubt. It permits revision. It changes when evidence changes. It requires effort and accepts incompleteness. A handed lens arrives finished. It offers certainty, belonging, and narrative relief. It reduces interpretive strain.

It can also reduce independence, because what arrives finished often discourages the harder work of looking again.

The handed lens often redirects attention rather than expanding it. It reframes structural realities as temporary misfortune or misdirected blame. It may encourage identification with hypothetical futures rather than present conditions. It can shift frustration laterally rather than vertically, preserving the curvature that produced the distortion in the first place. None of this requires overt deception. It requires only calibration that benefits the calibrator, while leaving the wearer convinced they are seeing for themselves.

Humans do not see with one eye. Depth perception requires convergence. Two separate inputs produce dimensional vision. The same principle applies cognitively. A single unexamined lens flattens complexity into one narrative track. Multiple lenses, handled properly, restore depth. Exposure to competing frames does not weaken perception when proportion is maintained. It strengthens it, because depth is not created by certainty alone but by comparison, tension, and correction.

Multiplicity is not confusion. It is calibration. Trying on lenses does not require surrendering judgment. It requires stability. The goal is not to accumulate contradiction but to test curvature. A stable mind can encounter opposing perspectives without dissolving into them. It can evaluate without absorbing. It can adjust without collapsing.

The horizon posture depends on maintained sight. Without preservation, lenses cloud. Without scrutiny, curvature hardens. Without multiplicity, depth collapses. No one hands you clarity intact. It must be preserved, examined, and recalibrated over time.

Chapter 4 Resolve

If you remember nothing else from this chapter, remember this:

Clarity is not permanent. Lenses must be preserved, examined, and recalibrated. When lenses are handed over unexamined or allowed to cloud through neglect, proportion contracts and depth collapses.

What This Chapter Is

An explanation of how cognitive lenses degrade through comfort, repetition, and neglect

A distinction between self-built lenses and pre-focused, handed lenses

A clarification of how multiplicity strengthens depth when proportion is maintained

A continuation of horizon orientation at the level of perception

What This Chapter Is Not

A claim that all shared frameworks are manipulative

A rejection of community, alignment, or tradition

An argument for permanent skepticism or isolation

A statement that individual perception is infallible

PART 2

The Disciplines That Stabilize Reality

THE DISCIPLINE OF PROPORTION

Why Stability Requires Restraint in an Age of Extremes

EXTREMES SIMPLIFY ORIENTATION BY collapsing complexity into binary positions. Refusing extremes requires sustained contact with tension that does not resolve cleanly. This chapter examines disciplined refusal as a stabilizing mechanism rather than a lack of conviction. Strength here is measured by maintained orientation under pressure, not by decisiveness alone.

This mechanism applies where conditions are multi-causal, contested, or resistant to binary framing. It governs environments where partial truths coexist and where action still depends on proportional judgment. It does not apply where conditions are genuinely binary or time-critical to the point that nuance collapses into immediacy. Refusal of extremes operates only when complexity is real and sustained engagement with it remains possible.

Refusing extremes is often misidentified as indecision, weakness, or avoidance. Indecision suspends judgment due to uncertainty or fear. Weakness avoids cost. Avoidance disengages. Disciplined refusal differs in that orientation is maintained while resisting premature closure. The mechanism does not deny conclusions; it delays collapse until sufficient alignment exists.

The distinction lies in continued contact with conditions rather than retreat from them. The middle is not the arithmetic average of two extremes. It means refusing to drop half of reality simply to feel certain. It is the discipline of holding multiple constraints simultaneously. Extremes simplify by collapsing tension. The middle preserves tension without allowing it to fracture judgment.

When people abandon the middle, they often believe they are choosing strength. In reality, they are choosing clarity over complexity. Extremes feel decisive because they remove competing obligations. The middle feels difficult because it refuses to discard them. Strength in the middle is not loud; it is stable. It absorbs pressure without amplifying it. It recognizes that reality rarely divides into clean moral halves and that sustainable decisions often require restraint rather than escalation.

The middle is not weakness; it is the refusal to drop half of reality to feel certain. It does not mean neutrality. It means proportion. Neutrality disengages. Proportion remains engaged but scaled. It evaluates claims based on evidence, consequence, and coherence rather than emotional velocity. This makes it slower, but it also makes it durable. In simple terms, neutrality steps away while proportion steps in carefully and deliberately.

When disciplined refusal erodes, extremes regain appeal by offering cognitive relief. Compression replaces proportion, and certainty substitutes for accuracy. Systems may begin to oscillate between opposing extremes rather than stabilize, mistaking movement for balance. Over time, refusal is reinterpreted as defect, and pressure increases to conform to simplified positions. As that pressure rises, the system's capacity to hold complex orientation without fracture diminishes.

Once the two dominant escape routes are visible, a familiar objection appears. If upward deferral and downward retreat both refuse responsibility, then rejecting them should imply strength. Yet many people reach the opposite conclusion. They assume that refusing extremes signals hesitation, compromise, or lack of conviction. In this view, strength requires total commitment, absolute belief, and unyielding posture. Anything less is framed as weakness. That assumption is false. Refusing extremes is not a failure of courage; it is a refusal to falsify reality.

The middle is often mistaken for dilution because intensity is confused with clarity. Extreme positions announce themselves loudly. They simplify complex systems into moral slogans. They divide the world into categories that require no maintenance, calibration, or patience. They offer certainty in exchange for alignment.

Living without escape offers none of these comforts. It does not eliminate ambiguity. It does not guarantee moral cleanliness. It does not promise belonging. Instead, it requires a person to remain present inside unresolved conditions. It demands action without total information. It requires decisions that are partial, revisable, and exposed to correction. That posture does not feel powerful; it feels vulnerable. This is why the middle is routinely mischaracterized. It does not numb discomfort or reward outrage. It does not allow a person to outsource failure to abstractions such as destiny, corruption, or lost golden ages. It keeps responsibility attached to outcomes.

Extreme positions feel strong because they remove ambiguity. When everything is framed as either righteous or corrupt, success and failure become impersonal. Responsibility migrates outward to enemies, systems, histories, or ideologies. Individual accountability dissolves into alignment. The middle refuses that relief. It insists on proportion. Proportion is demanding because it resists shortcuts. It requires distinguishing between mistake and malice, between breakdown and betrayal, between imperfection and collapse. These distinctions are not emotionally satisfying. They require attention, patience, and restraint.

Restraint is often mistaken for passivity. It is not. Restraint is an active discipline. It requires resisting impulses that feel righteous but produce instability. It requires holding competing truths without turning them into spectacle. It demands sustained engagement rather than dramatic release. This work is quiet, and quiet work is easy to overlook because it produces few symbols. It does not generate heroes or villains; it produces continuity.

Historically, societies are not preserved by those who pursue purity or certainty at all costs. They are preserved by those who keep systems functional despite imperfection. Maintenance, repair, and incremental correction do not inspire movements, but they prevent collapse. This does not make those people timid. It makes them responsible. The middle is not moral neutrality. It is moral constraint. Constraint recognizes limits—of knowledge, power, and human nature. It rejects the idea that good intentions absolve harm. It rejects the demand that human systems meet standards of purity they cannot satisfy. It rejects destruction disguised as courage.

Because of this, the middle attracts criticism from every direction. Those oriented toward upward escape accuse it of lacking vision or ambition. Those oriented toward backward escape accuse it of lacking authenticity or loyalty. Both critiques misunderstand its purpose. The middle is not trying to inspire belief. It is trying to preserve function. Functionality is rarely glamorous. It involves tradeoffs, ongoing maintenance, and acceptance of incomplete progress. It acknowledges that regression is always possible and that stability must be actively sustained. Yet functionality determines whether stress leads to adaptation or failure.

Refusal of extremes is not indecision. It is the decision to remain bound to reality even when reality is disappointing, incomplete, or slow to respond. Many abandon this posture not because they desire chaos, but because they mistake restraint for weakness and certainty for strength. Certainty feels solid. It is not. It is brittle.

Chapter 5 Resolve

If you remember nothing else from this chapter, remember this:

Refusing extremes preserves accountability and functional stability by keeping responsibility bound to reality.

What This Chapter Is

An explanation of why extreme positions feel strong while reducing accountability.

A description of how rejecting extremes maintains proportion and responsibility for outcomes.

A structural analysis of restraint as an active discipline rather than hesitation.

A claim about how functionality and continuity are preserved under imperfect conditions.

What This Chapter Is Not

An argument for moderation as compromise or indecisiveness.

A defense of moral neutrality or avoidance of judgment.

A claim about virtue, character superiority, or identity.

LITERACY AND SHARED REALITY

Why Reading Is the Infrastructure of Civilization

LITERACY FUNCTIONS AS AN interface between individual perception and shared systems. It enables accurate intake, comparison, and verification of information across time and distance. Without literacy, autonomy contracts and shared reality fragments. This chapter examines literacy as a structural mechanism rather than a cultural achievement. The mechanism applies to literacy as functional capacity: the ability to decode, interpret, and cross-reference symbolic information. It governs participation in systems that rely on written coordination, documentation, and abstraction. It does not apply to intelligence, creativity, or oral competence in isolation. Literacy here is not aesthetic fluency or credentialing; it is operational access to shared informational structures.

Literacy is frequently conflated with intelligence or education level. Intelligence may compensate locally but does not substitute for access to shared records. Education may credential without conferring functional literacy. Literacy specifically enables verification independent of authority or memory. The distinction matters because autonomy arises from the ability to check, compare, and revisit information, not from the ability to reason abstractly alone. Every functioning society depends on comprehension. This dependence is easy to overlook because, for those who read fluently, words disappear. Sentences convert into meaning without friction. Instructions are followed. Agreements are interpreted. Claims can be examined and compared.

When literacy weakens, nothing replaces it. This is not a claim about intelligence or effort. It is not a judgment about worth. It is a description of capacity. Literacy is the minimum equipment required to participate in a shared reality without constant mediation. Put plainly, if you cannot read carefully and consistently, someone else must read the world for you. Reading is not merely decoding symbols. It is the ability to track meaning across sentences, to hold definitions stable, to notice qualifiers, to distinguish assertion from evidence, and to recognize when language shifts midstream. These functions operate quietly until they fail. When they fail, autonomy contracts. A person who cannot read with precision cannot reliably consent. Medical instructions, legal terms, financial obligations, and civic rules become opaque. Understanding is outsourced to interpreters—formal or informal—whose interests may or may not align with the person relying on them.

Dependency increases without announcement. Low literacy does not simply limit information intake. It alters how information is processed. Long explanations become taxing. Conditional statements blur. Context drops out. What remains are fragments: headlines, slogans, repeated phrases, and emotionally charged cues. This is not a psychological flaw. It is a structural consequence. As comprehension weakens, interpretation becomes easier to steer. Language no longer constrains meaning; it becomes a vessel into which meaning can be poured. Ambiguity expands, and with it, the advantage of those who define terms.

Language is the load-bearing structure of coordination. Laws, norms, institutions, and trust all rely on shared definitions that persist across time and disagreement. When those definitions loosen, coordination degrades even when intentions remain intact. The result is not silence; it is noise. People begin using the same words to describe different things. Arguments proliferate without resolution because the terms under dispute are unstable. Disagreement intensifies not because positions are extreme, but because comprehension no longer overlaps. In this environment, force substitutes for understanding. Force may be social, economic, or procedural, but its role is the same: to settle what language no longer can.

Literacy is what allows disagreement without collapse. It permits claims to be slowed down, examined, and revised. It allows complexity to remain intact without being mistaken for evasion. It makes proportion possible by keeping distinctions visible: scope versus intent, error versus harm, limitation versus refusal. When literacy declines, simplification rushes in. Complex systems are reduced to singular causes. Multi-step processes are compressed into villains and heroes. Explanation is treated as excuse because following the explanation requires sustained attention that is no longer widely available.

This compression feeds the escape mechanisms already described. When comprehension demands effort, certainty becomes attractive. When paragraphs feel heavy, slogans feel light. Identity becomes easier than analysis because it requires no parsing and offers immediate belonging. The shift is subtle. It does not announce itself as ignorance. It presents as confidence without ballast.

A society experiencing this shift does not lose language. It loses shared meaning. Words continue to circulate, but they no longer anchor coordination. Each group carries its own definitions, and overlap narrows. At that point, shared reality fragments. Literacy functions as infrastructure. It allows meaning to travel intact across distance, time, and disagreement. Without it, systems still exist, but they cannot be jointly maintained because participants cannot reliably understand the same instructions, constraints, or consequences. Autonomy depends on this capacity. So does accountability. A person cannot be responsible for what they cannot comprehend, and a system cannot be legitimate if its terms cannot be read by those bound to them. These are not ethical claims. They are operational ones.

Where literacy is widespread, responsibility remains distributed because understanding is distributed. Where literacy erodes, responsibility migrates upward or outward, carried by specialists, interpreters, or authorities who become indispensable by default. This migration is rarely framed as loss. It often appears as efficiency or relief. But it alters the structure of participation. Fewer people can independently verify what is happening, and more must rely on trust without inspection.

Shared reality thins. This chapter does not argue for refinement or prestige. It describes a threshold. Below it, coordination becomes fragile. Above it, disagreement remains possible without disintegration. Literacy is the condition that allows people to inhabit the same horizon without collapsing into force or retreating into escape.

Chapter 6 Resolve

If you remember nothing else from this chapter, remember this:

Literacy is the capacity that allows people to understand shared rules and claims without intermediaries, making autonomy and coordination possible.

What This Chapter Is

An explanation of literacy as the functional ability to sustain shared meaning

A description of how comprehension enables consent, accountability, and nonviolent disagreement

A structural account of how declining literacy increases dependency and manipulability

An observation that coordination degrades when definitions and context cannot be held stable

What This Chapter Is Not

A claim about intelligence, effort, class, or personal worth

An argument for elitism, credentialism, or cultural refinement

A moral judgment about people with lower literacy

Competence Grounds Responsibility

Why Capability Precedes Authority

ABSTRACT SYSTEMS DEPEND ON concrete execution. Competence provides the connective tissue between design and function. When competence is absent, abstraction persists without support. This chapter examines competence as a sustaining mechanism that operates below visibility yet ultimately determines whether systems remain viable.

The mechanism applies to systems that require repeated execution over time: infrastructure, institutions, and coordinated processes. It governs maintenance, operation, and adaptation rather than initial conception. It does not apply to purely symbolic structures or one-time acts that do not require continuity. Competence matters wherever systems must endure beyond intent or design.

Competence is often confused with credentials, authority, or intelligence. Credentials may signal training without guaranteeing execution. Authority may direct without understanding. Intelligence may generate abstraction without implementation. Competence refers to reliable performance under real constraints. In simple terms, it means being able to actually do the thing rather than merely talk about it. The distinction lies in outcome consistency rather than conceptual sophistication or formal status.

When competence degrades, abstraction expands to fill the gap. Language, metrics, and intention proliferate to compensate for declining execution. Systems appear intact at the conceptual level while deteriorating operationally. Over time, the visibility of failure is delayed by layers of reporting, increasing the distance between perceived and actual function. Collapse, when it arrives, appears sudden despite the long erosion that preceded it.

Before culture became something people argued about, it was something people relied upon. Competence came first. Long before political identities, aesthetic tribes, or moral branding, culture functioned as a record of what worked. It accumulated through trial, failure, repair, and repetition. Knowledge survived because it reduced risk. Practices persisted because they produced stable outcomes. In this sense, culture was not expressive; it was operational. Competence was not ideological. It was necessary.

People learned how to build, repair, store, measure, navigate, and maintain because failure imposed immediate cost. A joint that failed collapsed a structure. A tool used incorrectly injured its user. A miscalculation spoiled a season's work. Errors did not remain abstract long enough to become opinions. They resolved into consequences.

This produced a form of discipline that required little external enforcement. Reality enforced it directly. Competence announced itself through results. Systems either held or they did not. Those who could keep things functioning were relied upon. Those who could not were corrected by necessity, taught through proximity, or removed from responsibility. Status followed reliability rather than assertion.

This was not a gentler time, but in many ways it was a clearer one. What mattered was not how an explanation sounded but whether a structure endured; not whether an intention was good but whether a process was sufficient. Skill earned trust because it reduced uncertainty for everyone involved.

As societies scaled, the relationship between action and outcome stretched. Systems grew larger, more layered, and more abstract. Feedback slowed. Failure became distributed across time and population. Under these conditions, competence became easier to mask. The shift was subtle. When consequences are delayed, obscured, or diffused, appearance can begin to substitute for performance. Language can replace understanding. Confidence can replace accuracy. People can participate in systems they do not comprehend and still appear functional. This is not a moral failure. It is a structural one.

Competence did not disappear because people stopped caring. Transparent feedback dissolved. The environment changed in a way that allowed people to operate without directly encountering the effects of their errors. Systems absorbed mistakes long enough to make them deniable. For a time, this compensation worked. Redundancy increased. Oversight multiplied.

Documentation expanded. Specialists carried growing burdens. Maintenance was postponed in order to preserve continuity. These adaptations kept systems running while concealing the erosion beneath them. But complexity cannot permanently replace competence.

As systems grow without corresponding understanding, fragility increases. Failures begin to appear in places no one expects. Breakdowns occur without clear causes. Repairs become reactive rather than restorative. Responsibility blurs because few people can explain how things work from beginning to end. Trust erodes not through cynicism but through repetition. People encounter systems that cannot be explained by those responsible for them. They experience outcomes no one can account for. Confidence weakens because reliability has weakened.

Predictable responses follow. Some turn backward, idealizing an earlier time when skill appeared more common, without accounting for the constraints and discipline that produced it. Others turn upward, substituting abstraction for capability and insisting that better intentions, narratives, or structures can compensate for missing proficiency. Neither response restores function.

Competence does not return through belief or declaration. It reappears through alignment with reality. It is rebuilt where understanding meets consequence and where responsibility remains attached to outcome. Competence does not require universal expertise. It requires sufficient understanding to recognize when something is failing and sufficient humility to defer to those who know more. It also requires systems to remain legible to the people who depend on them. This is not elitism. It is stewardship.

When a culture loses respect for competence, it becomes increasingly dependent on appearances. Authority drifts away from understanding. Outcomes are justified by intent. Failure is narrated rather than addressed. Over time, systems persist only because they have not yet been tested beyond their margin.

Competence forms the substrate beneath abstraction. Literacy enables shared meaning. Competence enables shared function. Where literacy allows people to understand what is being claimed, competence allows them to judge whether it can be done and whether it has been done well. Without competence, responsibility thins. Systems continue until they cannot. When failure finally becomes undeniable, repair becomes harder because the knowledge required to repair has already been lost.

Chapter 7 Resolve

If you remember nothing else from this chapter, remember this:

Competence is the practical capacity that keeps systems functioning as abstraction and scale increase.

What This Chapter Is

A description of how early culture formed around consequence-tested capability rather than expression or belief.

An explanation of how delayed and distributed feedback allows appearance to substitute for performance.

A structural account of how complexity temporarily compensates for declining competence while increasing fragility.

An observation that trust erodes when systems cannot be explained or reliably repaired by those responsible for them.

What This Chapter Is Not

A nostalgia claim that the past was better or easier.

An argument that expertise must be centralized or universal.

A moral judgment about intelligence, effort, or worth.

A policy proposal, reform agenda, or call to action.

Chapter Eight

Humility Preserves Learning

Why Intellectual Humility Protects Reality

Humility functions as a stabilizer for learning systems. It maintains openness to correction by preventing premature closure around self-assessment. When humility is absent, error becomes invisible rather than eliminated. This chapter examines humility as a structural mechanism that preserves adaptive capacity.

This mechanism applies to contexts where learning depends on feedback from conditions or other agents. It governs environments involving revision, iteration, and correction over time. It does not apply to situations where outcomes are fixed or where no feedback channel exists. Humility operates only where adjustment remains possible and where information can still enter the system.

Humility is often confused with self-doubt, deference, or lack of confidence. Self-doubt destabilizes judgment. Deference transfers responsibility. Lack of confidence impairs action. Humility differs in that it preserves agency while keeping orientation provisional. That means a person can act with confidence while still admitting adjustment may be necessary. The mechanism does not minimize competence; it prevents competence from becoming sealed against correction. The distinction lies in maintaining both action and receptivity at the same time.

When humility erodes, learning slows without appearing to stop. Feedback is reinterpreted as challenge or noise, and correction is reframed as threat. Errors persist longer because they are less likely to be acknowledged. Over time, the system narrows its intake while increasing internal certainty, reducing adaptability while preserving outward coherence.

When competence begins to matter again, a different failure mode appears. People confuse knowing things with being finished. Ignorance can be dangerous, but arrogance is worse. A person who knows little can still learn. A person who believes they already understand has closed the door. Learning does not stop because information is scarce; it stops because revision becomes socially costly. Pride in ignorance weakens societies. Pride in knowledge freezes them. Both replace learning with identity.

Modern culture often treats certainty as strength. Confidence is rewarded. Decisiveness is praised. Rhetorical dominance is mistaken for clarity. Admitting uncertainty is framed as weakness, and revising a position is treated as betrayal. Curiosity is tolerated only until it threatens alignment. This creates a perverse incentive structure. People stop asking questions not because answers are plentiful, but because inquiry becomes risky. Knowledge turns from a tool into a badge. Understanding is no longer pursued; it is performed. Agreement becomes safer than accuracy. This is how false confidence spreads.

A horizon-oriented posture treats knowledge differently. Knowing is provisional. Facts accumulate. Context shifts. Systems interact in ways no single observer fully grasps. Understanding is maintained through ongoing correction, not through arrival at a final position. This posture is disciplined, not timid.

Scientific work depends on it. Engineering reliability depends on it. Any system that survives stress does so because the people maintaining it are willing to acknowledge uncertainty, test assumptions, and revise conclusions. Correction is not a failure of confidence; it is evidence of function. Certainty feels powerful because it removes effort. Humility requires work.

Humility does not mean self-doubt. It means proportion. It means distinguishing between what is known, what is suspected, and what remains unclear. It keeps belief attached to evidence and identity detached from conclusions. When people become proud of knowing, they stop listening. When listening stops, error accumulates silently. By the time failure becomes visible, it is no longer small.

This is how intelligent societies make avoidable mistakes. Not through lack of intelligence, but through refusal to remain teachable. A culture that rewards performative certainty gradually loses its capacity for correction. Anomalies are ignored. Warnings are discounted. Messengers are attacked. Function continues on momentum until reality intervenes without negotiation.

The horizon posture resists this by separating identity from belief. A position can be held without becoming the person. A claim can be defended without being worshiped. Being wrong does not require collapse. This preserves learning under pressure. It allows disagreement to remain productive and evidence to retain authority. Correction can occur while costs are still low.

Competence keeps systems functional. Humility preserves the learning and correction that competence requires. Knowing is not the enemy. Believing you are finished knowing is.

Chapter 9 Resolve

If you remember nothing else from this chapter, remember this:

Pride in knowing shuts down learning by turning understanding into identity and blocking correction.

What This Chapter Is

An explanation of how confidence in having finished understanding stops learning

A description of how certainty becomes a social signal that replaces inquiry

A boundary claim about knowledge maintenance under complexity and stress, not about intelligence levels

An account of how suppressed correction allows errors to accumulate silently until failure surfaces

What This Chapter Is Not

An argument against expertise, knowledge, or education

A claim that uncertainty or indecision is preferable to judgment

A moral ranking of humble versus proud people

WORDS MEAN THINGS

Why Language Collapse Precedes Civilizational Collapse

LANGUAGE ENABLES COORDINATION BY stabilizing reference across individuals and across time. It anchors meaning sufficiently to permit planning, responsibility, and correction. When language destabilizes, coordination fragments. This chapter examines language as a structural anchor rather than merely an expressive tool.

The mechanism applies wherever coordination depends on shared reference, documentation, or explicit agreement. It governs systems that require repeatability, traceability, and accountability. It does not apply to purely expressive or private uses of language that make no claim to shared meaning. Language functions structurally when it binds actions to reference points that others can inspect.

Language is often conflated with rhetoric, persuasion, or expression. Rhetoric aims to influence. Expression conveys internal states. Structural language enables alignment independent of intent. The distinction matters because coordination depends on stable reference, not on emotional resonance or persuasive force. Confusing these roles erodes accountability by substituting impression for precision.

When language loses its anchoring function, terms begin to drift while appearing intact. Agreements become ambiguous without explicit revision. Accountability weakens as reference points dissolve. Systems continue to communicate, yet they lose the ability to coordinate action reliably or assign responsibility clearly. Breakdown occurs not through silence but through surplus language detached from stable meaning. Language is not decoration; it is infrastructure. Just as roads carry vehicles, words carry responsibility.

Language is not only a communication tool; it is also a compression system. Words carry accumulated definitions, histories, and boundaries. When those boundaries blur, accountability blurs with them. If "harm" expands to include discomfort, or "violence" expands to include disagreement, the scale of response becomes distorted. The erosion of language rarely begins as sabotage. It often begins as emotional urgency. A word is stretched to emphasize importance. Over time, repeated stretching weakens its structural integrity. When precision collapses, shared reality becomes negotiable.

In simple terms, when words lose edges, responsibility loses edges. Civilization depends on language remaining stable enough to adjudicate conflict. Laws, contracts, and moral claims rely on shared definitions. When definitions fragment, conflict escalates because parties are no longer arguing about events but about the meaning of the words describing them. If people cannot agree on what words mean, they cannot agree on what happened.

Words are the medium through which humans coordinate action, transmit knowledge, assign responsibility, and negotiate reality without force. They compress experience into shareable form. They make scale possible. For this reason, disputes about language are never merely semantic. When words lose precision, the systems that depend on them become unstable. This is a functional claim rather than a cultural one.

Clear language allows disagreement without chaos. It permits responsibility to be located accurately. It enables repair instead of perpetual accusation. When definitions drift, accountability thins. Ambiguity benefits power. When terms mean whatever is convenient in the moment, interpretation shifts to whoever has the loudest voice or the greatest leverage. Meaning stops being shared and becomes imposed. Confusion ceases to be accidental and becomes a tool.

As precision declines, conflict rises. People use identical words to describe different realities. Arguments escalate because participants are no longer responding to the same claims. Explanation gives way to accusation. Volume substitutes for clarity. At that point, disagreement no longer resolves through reasoning; it resolves through pressure—social, economic, or physical.

Language allows coordination at scale without coercion. Laws, contracts, standards, and institutions all rely on stable definitions. When language destabilizes, trust collapses and enforcement expands. This does not require language to be frozen.

Meanings can evolve and contexts can shift. But evolution requires continuity. Change must remain traceable, deliberate, and intelligible. Without continuity, learning breaks.

When language blurs, error cannot be named. People cannot correct mistakes if failures are linguistically obscured. Systems cannot be repaired if breakdowns are reframed as successes under altered definitions. Responsibility cannot attach if terms stretch to evade it. In this way, confusion spreads even without malicious intent.

Bad outcomes are rebranded as misunderstandings. Broken processes are described as progress. Rhetorical inflation replaces explanation. The appearance of motion substitutes for actual correction. A horizon-oriented posture resists this drift. It keeps words anchored to observable reality. It favors explanation over slogan and tolerates the discomfort that clarity requires. Precision is treated not as cruelty but as the means by which harm can be limited and repair remains possible.

Precision is not opposed to compassion. It is the condition that allows compassion to operate without blindness. Problems that cannot be described cannot be addressed. Harms that cannot be named cannot be contained. Language is the connective tissue binding literacy, competence, humility, and accountability. When it fails, they fail together.

Chapter 9 Resolve

If you remember nothing else from this chapter, remember this:

Language is the infrastructure that enables coordination and accountability at scale.

What This Chapter Is

A functional explanation of how language enables coordination, responsibility, and repair.

A description of how precision in definitions stabilizes systems and disagreement.

A boundary claim about language as operational infrastructure rather than expression or culture.

An account of how ambiguity concentrates power and dissolves accountability.

What This Chapter Is Not

A political or cultural critique of specific groups or movements.

A demand to freeze language or resist linguistic change.

A moral judgment about good people versus bad people.

PART 3

The Structures That Sustain Civilization

CIVILIZATION IS A RELAY RACE

Why Each Generation Maintains What It Did Not Build

CIVILIZATION PERSISTS THROUGH TRANSMISSION rather than spontaneous creation. Each generation receives structures, practices, and knowledge formed prior to individual participation. When inheritance is obscured, systems misattribute stability to present action alone. This chapter examines inheritance as a structural condition of civilization.

The mechanism applies to systems that extend beyond individual lifespans and require accumulated knowledge or infrastructure. It governs institutions, norms, and technical capacities transmitted over time. It does not apply to isolated acts or short-lived arrangements that do not rely on prior accumulation. Inheritance operates where continuity exceeds individual contribution.

Inheritance is often confused with entitlement, nostalgia, or authority. Entitlement assumes guaranteed access. Nostalgia idealizes the past. Authority enforces continuity. Inheritance, in this context, describes structural dependence on prior work regardless of valuation. The distinction lies in recognizing transmission as a condition, not as a moral claim or emotional attachment.

When inheritance is ignored, maintenance appears optional and transmission weakens. Systems consume accumulated capacity without replenishment, mistaking residual function for self-sufficiency. Over time, degradation accelerates as knowledge and infrastructure decay faster than they are restored. Collapse is often interpreted as sudden despite long-term erosion of inherited supports.

Civilization does not reset with each generation. That may sound obvious, yet much contemporary thinking behaves as if it were untrue. People are encouraged—often implicitly—to experience themselves as self-originating, as though they entered the world unburdened by what came before and unaccountable to what follows. This posture feels liberating. It is also inaccurate.

Every human life begins inside systems that were already built: roads and grids, tools and standards, languages and laws, methods of production, habits of cooperation, and accumulated knowledge. These systems did not arise spontaneously. They were assembled, tested, repaired, and handed forward by people who are no longer present.

No one earns their starting position. They inherit it. You begin your life on a track that was already built. This is not a moral claim. It is a structural one. Civilization functions as continuity, not as personal achievement. It persists only if each generation understands itself as temporary custodian rather than final author.

The relay race captures this structure. In a relay, no runner creates the track. No runner designs the baton. No runner completes the race alone. Each runner's role is bounded but real: receive the baton intact, run their segment competently, and pass it forward without dropping it. Dropping the baton does not primarily penalize the runner who drops it. It penalizes everyone who runs after. This is the geometry of civilization across time.

Modern culture often attempts to replace this geometry with narratives of self-expression, reinvention, or generational rupture. Questioning inheritance is not itself an error. Inherited systems can be flawed, incomplete, or unjust. But when questioning severs responsibility rather than clarifying it, continuity collapses. The resulting illusion is that inheritance is optional. It is not.

Infrastructure degrades without maintenance. Institutions fail without stewardship. Knowledge erodes when it is not transmitted. Norms dissolve when they are neither reinforced nor revised. None of this requires hostility or intent. Neglect is sufficient. This is how civilizations weaken without spectacle. Systems continue to operate, but fewer people understand how they function or feel accountable for preserving them. Maintenance becomes invisible. Repair becomes contentious. Stewardship becomes discretionary. Failure then appears sudden, even though it has been accumulating quietly for years.

A horizon-oriented society rejects the fantasy of self-origination. It recognizes inheritance as unavoidable and responsibility as structural rather than elective. This recognition does not demand reverence for the past. It demands accuracy about dependence. Reform requires continuity. Improvement requires comprehension of what is being altered. Progress that denies inheritance does not build forward. It consumes what already exists.

Chapter 10 Resolve

If you remember nothing else from this chapter, remember this:

Civilization persists only through inherited systems that require continuous stewardship across generations.

What This Chapter Is

An explanation of civilization as a continuity system rather than a self-originating achievement

A description of inheritance as a structural condition, not a moral choice

A boundary claim applying to shared systems across time, not individual worth or intent

An account of how neglect alone degrades systems without collapse or malice

What This Chapter Is Not

A rejection of reform, critique, or revision of inherited systems

A claim that the past was just, sufficient, or should be preserved unchanged

A judgment about individuals, generations, or identities

OBLIGATION DOES NOT END WITH YOU

Why Responsibility Extends Across Generations

OBLIGATION OPERATES INDEPENDENTLY OF individual preference or immediate benefit. It arises from participation in shared systems that impose requirements regardless of personal salience. When obligation is reduced to relevance, system coherence degrades. This chapter examines obligation as a structural condition rather than a motivational state.

This mechanism applies where systems rely on contributions or constraints that are not continuously negotiated at the individual level. It governs civic, institutional, and interdependent arrangements that persist regardless of personal alignment. It does not apply to voluntary affiliations that can be exited without consequence. Obligation functions where participation itself generates requirements beyond personal interest.

Obligation is often confused with coercion, loyalty, or moral agreement. Coercion imposes compliance through force. Loyalty reflects emotional attachment. Moral agreement implies shared values. Obligation, as used here, arises structurally from system participation, not from consent or sentiment. The distinction matters because obligations persist even when enthusiasm, agreement, or identification diminishes.

When obligation collapses into personal relevance, compliance becomes intermittent and selective. Systems adapt by increasing enforcement or narrowing scope, which reduces resilience over time. Shared functions begin to degrade as participation becomes conditional on alignment. Breakdown then appears as conflict over fairness rather than as erosion of the underlying structures of obligation.

One of the quiet assumptions of modern life is that responsibility becomes optional once it stops being personal. This assumption appears in many forms, but it usually reduces to the same claim: if something does not directly affect me, if I did not choose it, or if I will not be here to experience the outcome, then my obligation is limited. The claim feels reasonable. It is also corrosive.

Responsibility is not defined by proximity. It is defined by participation. People participate in systems they did not design. They benefit from decisions they did not make. They rely on structures that were built, maintained, and protected by others who expected no recognition from them. That participation exists regardless of awareness or consent.

Participation produces obligation whether it is acknowledged or not. If you benefit from a system, you are already part of it. Many attempts to avoid this obligation rely on narrowing its scope. Responsibility is reframed as something owed only to family, private projects, or immediate interests. Everything else is treated as optional, abstract, or someone else's concern.

Civilization does not function on private responsibility alone. It functions on shared obligation, on the willingness of people to care for outcomes that extend beyond personal relevance, immediate reward, or individual lifespan. This is easiest to see by looking backward rather than forward.

Most systems that support modern life were not built by people who received their full benefit. Infrastructure, public health standards, legal continuity, technical knowledge, and institutional memory were developed incrementally, often under uncertainty, often at personal cost, and often without assurance that the effort would succeed.

If responsibility had been limited to immediate payoff or personal relevance, those systems would not exist. When obligation is treated as optional beyond the self, the result is not neutrality. It is extraction. Benefits continue to be drawn from shared systems while responsibility for their condition is disclaimed. The system absorbs the cost until it can no longer do so quietly.

A horizon-oriented society recognizes that obligation scales with impact. When actions shape conditions others must live within, responsibility follows, independent of intent, belief, or identity. This does not imply total responsibility. No one is accountable for everything.

But responsibility does not disappear simply because consequences are delayed, distributed, or inherited by others. Obligation does not require self-negation or moral heroics. It requires proportion, a constraint that prevents decisions from knowingly degrading shared conditions simply because the cost will arrive later or fall elsewhere.

When this constraint is rejected, it is often justified using the language of freedom, authenticity, or realism. Yet freedom that ignores consequence does not reduce constraint; it displaces it onto others. Authenticity that rejects responsibility does not preserve honesty; it converts preference into entitlement.

A society that normalizes indifference to shared outcomes gradually loses the capacity to produce shared goods. Trust thins. Cooperation becomes conditional. Systems are expected to absorb strain without maintenance, correction, or stewardship. This does not produce collapse. It produces fragmentation.

Civilization persists not only through belief, competence, or language, but through the acceptance that obligation extends beyond comfort, convenience, and personal horizon. Without that acceptance, continuity degrades even when no one intends harm.

Chapter 11 Resolve

If you remember nothing else from this chapter, remember this:

Responsibility is created by participation in shared systems, not by personal relevance or proximity.

What This Chapter Is

An explanation of how obligation arises from participation in shared systems

A description of how narrowing responsibility to personal relevance enables extraction

A structural account of why shared obligation is required for civilization to persist

An analysis of how delayed or distributed consequences still carry responsibility

What This Chapter Is Not

A demand for self-sacrifice, altruism, or moral heroism

A claim that individuals are responsible for all outcomes or all systems

A moral judgment about good or bad people

Conflict Must Be Contained, Not Eliminated

Why Civilization Requires Managed Tension

Conflict emerges naturally from divergence within shared systems. Its elimination is neither feasible nor stabilizing. Containment allows systems to absorb disagreement without disintegration. This chapter examines containment as the functional response to persistent conflict.

The mechanism applies wherever multiple agents interact within shared constraints and interests cannot be fully aligned. It governs political, organizational, and social systems that must persist despite disagreement. It does not apply to isolated tasks or homogeneous environments where conflict does not structurally arise. Containment presupposes ongoing interaction rather than final resolution.

Containment is often confused with suppression, avoidance, or resolution. Suppression forces silence without addressing tension. Avoidance disengages. Resolution seeks closure. Containment differs in that conflict remains present but bounded. The distinction lies in preserving system integrity while allowing disagreement to exist without dominating function.

When containment fails, conflict expands beyond its original scope. Disagreement migrates into unrelated domains and begins to overwhelm coordination. Systems polarize as boundaries dissolve, and escalation replaces management. Attempts to eliminate conflict intensify it, while avoidance allows tension to accumulate. Stability erodes as conflict becomes the organizing principle rather than a managed condition.

Conflict is not a malfunction of social life. It is a predictable consequence of people sharing space, resources, authority, and time. Wherever priorities differ and tradeoffs exist, friction appears. The presence of conflict does not indicate collapse. The absence of conflict would indicate stasis, coercion, or silence. What determines whether conflict is survivable is not its intensity but its containment. In other words, disagreement itself is not the danger; the absence of boundaries is. Conflict becomes dangerous when it is allowed to spread without limit, without process, and without any agreed structure to absorb its force.

In functioning systems, conflict is bounded. It occurs within shared rules, stable language, and recognized roles. Disagreement can be sharp without becoming destructive because the framework that holds it remains intact. Participants may lose arguments without losing standing. Outcomes may disappoint without dissolving legitimacy. That boundedness is what allows conflict to remain part of the system rather than becoming a threat to the system itself.

When containment weakens, conflict changes form. Disagreement no longer tests claims; it tests endurance. Arguments cease to focus on resolving tradeoffs and instead become contests over who absorbs cost. Language shifts from diagnosis to accusation. Process is treated as obstruction rather than protection. The structure that once absorbed disagreement becomes the target of disagreement. Once that happens, every dispute begins pushing against the frame instead of remaining inside it.

At this stage, conflict stops functioning as a corrective mechanism and begins operating as a transfer mechanism. Burden is pushed outward. Responsibility is displaced. Losses are reframed as injustice inflicted by others rather than consequences emerging from shared systems. Escalation follows even without deliberate malice. People may still believe they are defending fairness while they are actually stripping away the conditions that make fairness manageable.

If rules are viewed as optional, bypassing them appears efficient. If competence is scarce, improvisation substitutes for repair. If obligation is denied, consequences are interpreted as external aggression. Each step increases pressure on the remaining structures, which are then blamed for failing under loads they were never designed to carry without maintenance. The system is treated as both expendable and responsible at the same time.

Attempts to eliminate conflict under these conditions accelerate failure. Suppressing disagreement does not restore containment; it removes feedback. Enforcing unanimity does not produce stability; it converts unresolved tension into latent force. The system may appear calm while accumulating stress it can no longer process incrementally. What looks like peace in those moments is often only compression.

Containment, by contrast, allows conflict to exist without consuming the system that hosts it. Containment does not require agreement. It requires boundaries. It depends on shared definitions, recognizable procedures, and the expectation that disputes occur inside the system rather than against it. Losses are tolerated because participation continues. Authority may be challenged without being erased. Correction remains possible because the framework persists. That persistence matters because systems survive not by eliminating friction, but by keeping friction from becoming the primary organizing force.

When containment erodes, power fills the gap. The strongest actors, through leverage, position, or influence, begin shaping outcomes directly. Coordination gives way to coercion. Persuasion loses relevance because rules no longer constrain advantage. What appears as increasing polarization is often a symptom of uncontained conflict rather than its cause. The visible hostility is real, but it is not the first failure. The first failure was the weakening of the structures that once kept hostility bounded.

By the time this shift becomes visible, it is commonly misdiagnosed. Disagreement itself is blamed. Passion is treated as the threat. People search for ways to quiet voices instead of recognizing that the structures which once allowed voices to coexist have thinned. Conflict did not break the system. The loss of containment did.

Chapter 12 Resolve

If you remember nothing else from this chapter, remember this:

Conflict becomes destructive only when the structures that contain it fail.

What This Chapter Is

An explanation of why conflict is a normal condition of shared systems rather than a sign of breakdown.

A description of containment as the structural boundary that allows disagreement without system damage.

An account of how weakened rules, language, and roles transform conflict from correction into cost transfer.

An observation that escalation emerges from the loss of containment rather than increased hostility.

What This Chapter Is Not

A claim that disagreement is dangerous or should be minimized.

An argument for harmony, consensus, or suppression of opposing views.

A moral judgment about who is right, wrong, virtuous, or corrupt.

REPAIR IS NOT ROMANTIC

Why Maintenance Sustains What Ideals Alone Cannot

CIVILIZATIONAL CONTINUITY DEPENDS ON ongoing repair rather than episodic achievement. Visible successes draw attention, but it is invisible maintenance and repair that preserve function over time. When repair is neglected, systems decay despite periodic display. This chapter examines repair as a sustaining mechanism distinct from innovation or performance.

The mechanism applies to systems subject to wear, entropy, or cumulative error. It governs infrastructure, institutions, and practices requiring regular correction. It does not apply to static artifacts or one-time outputs that do not degrade through use. Repair operates where continuity depends on ongoing intervention.

Repair is often conflated with improvement, reform, or spectacle. Improvement aims to advance capability. Reform restructures systems. Spectacle signals success. Repair restores function to existing structures. The distinction matters because repair preserves continuity, whereas improvement and reform may disrupt it. Confusing these roles leads to neglect of foundational maintenance.

When repair is undervalued, deterioration proceeds unnoticed beneath visible activity. Some failures do not reverse quickly. A bridge can be rebuilt in months. A water system can take decades. A skilled workforce can take a generation. Public trust can take longer than either. Recovery time is not determined by intention. It is determined by how long the damage was allowed to accumulate. Systems can appear dynamic while losing reliability underneath. Failures begin to cluster as small defects accumulate without correction. Eventually, repair costs escalate or become infeasible, and collapse appears abrupt despite a prolonged period of neglected maintenance.

Civilizations do not fail because they choose hard options. They fail because they delay until only bad options remain. Early decisions are uncomfortable but flexible. Late decisions are unavoidable and expensive. Leadership is not always choosing a good path. Sometimes it is choosing the least damaging one that remains. Delay does not preserve options. Delay removes them.

Once conflict is understood as survivable when contained, another distinction becomes visible. Breakdown is not caused by a lack of declaration. It emerges when repair recedes from view. Systems do not usually fail because no one spoke. They fail because fewer and fewer people remained willing to do the unglamorous work of correction.

Repair does not resemble resolution. It does not arrive as a moment or a turning point. It appears as repeated adjustment inside existing structures. Its effects are cumulative rather than dramatic, and its presence is often visible only in hindsight, when systems continue to function instead of collapsing. Because repair lacks spectacle, it is often misread as stagnation.

Public attention tends to reward rupture. Language, status, and recognition flow toward events that feel decisive. Repair produces none of these signals. It operates through continuity rather than contrast. As a result, it is frequently treated as secondary, deferred, or invisible. Yet systems persist through repair, not declaration. They endure because someone keeps absorbing friction that no headline will ever celebrate.

Civilizations do not deteriorate primarily from disagreement or error. They deteriorate when small failures are allowed to remain unreconciled, when misalignments accumulate without correction, and when maintenance is postponed in favor of symbolic action. Over time, unresolved strain becomes structural weakness.

Repair functions inside constraint. It does not begin from blank space. It works within inherited designs, partial solutions, and imperfect components. It adjusts what exists rather than replacing it wholesale. This makes repair resistant to simplification and incompatible with purity narratives. Where spectacle seeks coherence, repair tolerates inconsistency. It accepts that continuity often depends on working with flawed materials rather than waiting for ideal ones.

Repair accepts that systems can function while remaining flawed, and that improvement often arrives unevenly. It neither sanctifies what exists nor treats it as irredeemable. Instead, it remains oriented toward function under real conditions. This posture creates discomfort. It denies the emotional relief that comes from either romanticizing the old or fantasizing about total replacement.

Repair offers progress without absolution. It does not resolve responsibility through moral clarity or rhetorical certainty. It keeps accountability attached to outcomes rather than intentions. The work continues even when recognition does not. In this sense, repair is disciplined precisely because it refuses the luxury of symbolic completion.

As repair recedes, commentary expands. Diagnosis multiplies while correction slows. Naming failure becomes easier than absorbing the friction of adjustment. Over time, the act of identification begins to substitute for improvement, and explanation replaces stewardship. This substitution feels active while remaining inert. The appearance of engagement starts masking the absence of maintenance.

Repair, by contrast, concentrates responsibility. It forces engagement with how systems actually operate, where strain accumulates, and which failures matter most. It does not permit distance, because distance dissolves accountability. Civilizations endure not because they avoid failure, but because repair remains present long after attention has moved elsewhere.

When repair is treated as optional or beneath notice, decay does not arrive suddenly. It advances quietly, through neglected interfaces, deferred corrections, and unowned maintenance. Collapse is only the final visible stage of a long period without repair.

Repair is never optional. It is not inspirational. It is structural. It is the quiet work that keeps everything from falling apart.

Chapter 13 Resolve

If you remember nothing else from this chapter, remember this:

Civilizations persist through continuous repair within existing structures, not through declarations or spectacle.

What This Chapter Is

An explanation of how systems endure through repeated adjustment rather than decisive moments

A description of repair as cumulative correction operating inside inherited constraints

A boundary claim applying to ongoing system function, not crisis response or replacement events

An account of how neglected repair allows small failures to accumulate into structural weakness

What This Chapter Is Not

A critique of disagreement, dissent, or conflict as causes of breakdown

An argument for preserving all existing systems regardless of performance

A moral judgment about virtue, effort, or intent

SCALE DEMANDS GOVERNANCE, NOT MORAL SHORTCUTS

Why Large Systems Require Structure

AS SYSTEMS INCREASE IN scale, informal regulation loses effectiveness. Coordination across distance, volume, and time requires structured control mechanisms. Moral impulse alone cannot substitute for governance at scale. This chapter examines governance as the functional requirement imposed by scale.

This mechanism applies where systems exceed the capacity of direct personal oversight. It governs large organizations, populations, and infrastructures where interactions multiply beyond individual control. It does not apply to small-scale or short-lived arrangements where informal norms can regulate behavior directly. Governance emerges as a necessity only when scale introduces complexity that cannot be managed relationally.

Governance is often confused with morality, intent, or virtue signaling. Morality guides individual judgment. Intent reflects purpose. Virtue signaling communicates alignment. Governance structures behavior through rules, processes, and accountability independent of individual character. The distinction matters because moral consensus cannot reliably coordinate large systems without formal mechanisms.

When governance is replaced by moral shortcuts, enforcement becomes inconsistent. Rules are applied selectively, and authority shifts toward perception rather than structure. Systems rely on signaling instead of process, increasing arbitrariness. Over time, trust erodes as outcomes appear disconnected from declared principles, destabilizing coordination under scale.

Human judgment evolved at a scale where causes and effects are close together. What works in a family does not automatically work in a nation, and what stabilizes a nation must still protect families within it. A decision is made, a response is seen, and correction follows quickly. Faces are visible. Consequences arrive within the span of attention. Responsibility feels tangible because feedback is immediate.

This intuition remains reliable in small domains. Families, crews, classrooms, and local workplaces all operate within ranges where personal judgment can track outcomes without much distortion. Promises can be kept or broken in ways that are legible. Harm can be traced. Repair can be directed. As systems grow, this alignment loosens.

Scale separates action from effect. Distance increases. Time stretches. Participation multiplies. What was once a single decision becomes a chain of procedures. What was once a visible outcome becomes an aggregate. Responsibility diffuses across roles, organizations, and years. At that point, intuition begins to misfire.

People continue to apply personal moral reasoning to environments that no longer provide personal feedback. They expect clarity from structures that are inherently probabilistic. They interpret delayed outcomes as evasion. They treat distributed responsibility as denial rather than as a structural property of scale. What feels evasive is often structural distance. What feels impersonal is often simply the shape of a large system.

Others respond by detaching entirely. Large systems are treated as forces rather than constructions. Outcomes are framed as inevitable. Responsibility is dissolved into complexity. The system is described, but no one is seen to be accountable for its behavior.

Both responses share a common error. They attempt to resolve scale through moral compression rather than through governance. Moral compression reduces complex operations into emotionally legible positions. It converts systemic behavior into narratives of virtue or vice. It assigns blame or praise without tracing mechanisms. It produces coherence by ignoring structure.

This works rhetorically. It fails operationally. At scale, systems persist or fail based on constraints, feedback loops, role clarity, and enforcement of limits. None of these can be replaced by moral alignment alone. Values may inform priorities, but they do not execute. They may guide a system, but they cannot by themselves operate one.

Governance exists because intuition does not scale. Governance is not an ideology. It is the set of structures that allow large numbers of people to coordinate without relying on shared intent or constant agreement. It establishes boundaries within which disagreement can occur without collapse. It allocates authority so that decisions can be made even when consensus is unavailable. It defines accountability so that correction remains possible when outcomes drift.

When governance is weak, moral shortcuts proliferate. One shortcut is personalization. Systemic outcomes are attributed to individual character. Success is treated as proof of virtue. Failure is treated as evidence of malice. Structural factors are minimized because they complicate the story. Attention focuses on visible figures rather than on process.

Another shortcut is abstraction. Responsibility is pushed upward into concepts. Decisions are justified by appeals to necessity, history, or inevitability. Human agency disappears into scale. Correction is deferred because no clear locus of action can be identified.

Both shortcuts reduce discomfort. Neither stabilizes systems. Scale introduces tradeoffs that cannot be resolved by moral purity. Resources are finite. Time is constrained. Actions taken to reduce one risk often increase another. Governance exists to manage these tensions without pretending they do not exist. This management is procedural, not inspirational. It relies on rules that persist beyond individual conviction. It requires mechanisms that operate even when participants disagree or disengage. It accepts imperfection as a condition rather than as a failure.

At scale, outcomes matter independently of intent. Intent remains relevant to individual conduct, but systems are judged by behavior under stress. A structure that performs well only when staffed by unusually competent or benevolent individuals is fragile. A structure that degrades gracefully under ordinary conditions exhibits governance. This distinction is often resisted because it removes the comfort of moral self-assessment. It replaces declarations with measurement. It replaces alignment with constraint.

Scale also changes the nature of responsibility.

Responsibility does not disappear as systems grow; it relocates. It attaches to roles rather than to persons. It persists across time rather than within moments. It becomes less visible but more consequential. When roles are unclear, responsibility thins. When authority is informal, accountability becomes selective. When correction depends on goodwill, errors accumulate. Governance formalizes responsibility so that it survives turnover, disagreement, and fatigue. It creates continuity where intuition would otherwise reset with each new participant.

Moral shortcuts undermine this continuity. They privilege urgency over durability. They reward expression over execution. They substitute condemnation for correction. They intensify conflict without improving coordination.

At scale, conflict cannot be eliminated, but it can be contained. Governance provides containment by channeling disagreement into defined processes. When those processes are bypassed in favor of moral escalation, conflict expands beyond its corrective function and begins to consume the system itself.

This is why scale produces recurring patterns of dysfunction even among populations that broadly share values. Shared values do not produce shared outcomes without shared governance. Agreement does not substitute for structure.

As systems grow, legitimacy also shifts. In small groups, legitimacy emerges from familiarity and trust. At scale, legitimacy depends on predictability. People accept outcomes they dislike when processes are stable, roles are clear, and correction is possible. They resist outcomes they might otherwise tolerate when decision paths are opaque or inconsistent. Governance sustains legitimacy by making behavior legible. Moral shortcuts obscure behavior by framing outcomes as moral verdicts rather than as system results.

Scale exposes another limitation of intuition: proportionality. Personal judgment is binary by default. Actions feel right or wrong. Systems operate on gradients. Small deviations can be acceptable. Large deviations may be catastrophic. Governance establishes thresholds, tolerances, and escalation paths that intuition alone cannot reliably maintain.

Without these, systems oscillate between overreaction and neglect. Moral framing amplifies this oscillation. It treats every deviation as a crisis or dismisses accumulated deviation until collapse forces attention. Governance moderates response by separating signal from noise. This separation is procedural. It depends on monitoring, reporting, and correction mechanisms that persist regardless of sentiment.

As scale increases, the cost of moral shortcuts rises. What feels clarifying at the level of rhetoric becomes destabilizing at the level of operation. Systems lose their ability to absorb error. Coordination gives way to alignment tests. Enforcement becomes inconsistent. Trust erodes not because values differ, but because behavior becomes unpredictable.

Governance does not resolve disagreement. It prevents disagreement from becoming disintegration.

It does so by constraining power, formalizing responsibility, and preserving channels for correction. These functions are unglamorous. They rarely produce emotional satisfaction. They operate beneath attention.

When governance is replaced by moral shortcuts, systems remain active for a time. Complexity can mask deterioration. Momentum carries function forward. Eventually, however, uncorrected drift accumulates. Failures become harder to diagnose because responsibility is unclear and language has polarized.

At that point, calls for more moral intensity increase. The shortcut is applied again with greater force. The system weakens further.

Scale demands governance because it removes the feedback that intuition relies upon. Moral shortcuts attempt to restore that feedback symbolically. They substitute feeling for function.

A horizon-oriented posture recognizes this limit. It distinguishes between personal conduct and systemic design. It accepts that large systems require rule-based coordination to remain humane. It treats governance as maintenance, not as moral theater.

Where intuition ends, structure begins. Where structure is absent, moral shortcuts rush in. Where shortcuts dominate, systems drift until failure becomes unavoidable.

Chapter 14 Resolve

If you remember nothing else from this chapter, remember this:

At scale, systems remain stable only through governance because moral intuition and value signaling cannot coordinate outcomes without structure.

What This Chapter Is

An explanation of why personal moral intuition breaks down as systems grow in size, distance, and duration

A description of how moral shortcuts replace governance when feedback weakens

A boundary claim applying to large, multi-participant systems rather than small interpersonal settings

An account of how governance preserves coordination, accountability, and legitimacy under scale

What This Chapter Is Not

An argument against morality, values, or personal ethics

A claim that large systems eliminate responsibility or human agency

A moral judgment about good or bad people

A policy proposal, solution set, or call to action

GOVERNANCE IS NOT SALVATION

Why Institutions Stabilize Power but Do Not Redeem It

GOVERNANCE ENABLES COORDINATION BUT does not resolve all system tensions. It functions instrumentally rather than redemptively. Treating governance as salvation distorts both its use and the expectations placed upon it. This chapter examines governance as a constrained tool operating within broader system limits.

The mechanism applies to governance structures designed to manage behavior, allocate resources, or enforce rules. It governs procedural control rather than moral outcome. It does not apply to personal transformation or cultural meaning-making. Governance operates where structure can shape interaction, not where resolution depends on internal change.

Governance is often conflated with legitimacy, justice, or final authority. Legitimacy concerns acceptance. Justice concerns fairness. Final authority implies ultimate resolution. Governance provides mechanisms for coordination and constraint, not moral completion. The distinction matters because it prevents governance from being overloaded with expectations it cannot meet without distortion.

When governance is treated as salvific, expansion accelerates beyond functional limits. Rules proliferate in an effort to address problems that are not structural, increasing complexity without resolving the underlying tension. Disillusionment follows when outcomes fail to match inflated expectations. Governance then becomes brittle, criticized for shortcomings that arise less from design failure than from being misapplied.

When scale overwhelms intuition and repair becomes unavoidable, people often begin looking for a final answer. They look for governance to save them. That impulse is understandable because governance provides visible structure in moments of uncertainty. The presence of rules can feel like protection, even when those rules cannot resolve the deeper tension that produced the uncertainty in the first place.

Governance is not redemption. It is not a moral reset, and it is not proof of virtue. Governance is a tool, necessary, limited, and fragile, designed to manage shared systems when individual action alone cannot. It can organize responsibility, but it cannot replace individual human character or judgment. It can constrain behavior. It cannot redeem motive.

Confusing governance with salvation produces two symmetrical failures that reinforce each other over time. One failure expands governance beyond its limits, while the other rejects governance entirely. Both reactions emerge from frustration with imperfect outcomes rather than from a clear understanding of governance itself.

One side treats governance as a substitute for responsibility. If the right rules exist, the thinking goes, outcomes will take care of themselves. Personal discipline, competence, and judgment become secondary to compliance. Engagement declines because responsibility appears to have been transferred to the system. The person obeys and then imagines the obligation is complete.

The other side treats governance as illegitimate by default. Any constraint is framed as tyranny, and any coordination is framed as control. The need for shared rules is denied in favor of individual preference. Authority is resisted even when coordination is necessary to preserve stability. Freedom is redefined as the absence of structure rather than the ability to function within it.

Both positions collapse under pressure because neither reflects how complex systems actually function. A society without governance fragments as coordination fails. A society that treats governance as sacred becomes rigid and unresponsive to changing conditions. Effective governance holds the middle by recognizing both necessity and limitation.

It accepts that rules are required when systems exceed personal scale. It also accepts that rules cannot replace judgment, competence, or moral agency. Governance does not absolve people of responsibility; it organizes responsibility so that action remains coordinated across time and distance. It creates channels. It does not create virtue.

Governance fails when it becomes performative rather than functional. Rules written to signal values rather than manage reality accumulate quickly and decay just as fast. They create compliance theater without improving outcomes. Trust erodes because people sense the widening gap between language and effect. When that gap grows large enough, even necessary rules begin losing legitimacy through association.

Good governance is rarely dramatic because it focuses on constraint rather than display. It concentrates on incentives, boundaries, and failure modes rather than ideals. It anticipates misuse, assumes error, and plans for human inconsistency. This orientation does not make governance cynical. It makes governance durable.

A horizon-oriented society treats governance as maintenance infrastructure rather than moral theater. It evaluates rules by how well they reduce harm, preserve function, and survive stress. It does not measure governance by emotional satisfaction or symbolic clarity. Durability, not inspiration, becomes the standard of success.

Governance also requires limits because no system can solve problems it was not designed to address. When governance is asked to deliver meaning, identity, or moral purity, it inevitably overreaches. Complexity increases while clarity declines. The system becomes burdened with expectations it cannot fulfill. It is then judged not for what it was built to do, but for what people wished it could do.

The result is backlash, avoidance, and eventual breakdown as people lose confidence in the system's capacity to function. Criticism intensifies because the expectations were unrealistic from the beginning. Governance appears to fail even when the underlying design remains sound. In that sense, misexpectation becomes its own kind of sabotage.

This dynamic matters because many people place impossible expectations on governance while simultaneously refusing the personal and cultural discipline that governance depends on. Systems require participation as well as structure. Without both, coordination weakens regardless of how many rules exist. Procedure cannot carry a culture that refuses every burden not immediately enforced.

When governance is expected to save people from themselves, it grows coercive as enforcement expands to compensate for declining responsibility. When governance is rejected outright, power fills the vacuum informally through influence, leverage, or force. Neither outcome preserves freedom or stability. Both simply relocate domination into different forms.

The next chapter returns to the individual not as a hero or a villain, but as the smallest unit of civilization. It asks what it actually means to live well within imperfect systems that cannot deliver redemption but can still preserve continuity.

Because institutions cannot save orientation, the responsibility returns to posture.

Chapter 15 Resolve

If you remember nothing else from this chapter, remember this:

Governance is a limited coordination tool that organizes responsibility at scale and cannot replace judgment, competence, or moral agency.

What This Chapter Is

A structural explanation of what governance is and why it exists when systems exceed personal scale

An analysis of how governance organizes responsibility rather than absolving it

A description of two symmetrical failure modes: treating governance as salvation or rejecting it entirely

A boundary statement defining governance as maintenance infrastructure with design limits

An observation that performative governance erodes trust by signaling values instead of managing reality

What This Chapter Is Not

An argument for expanding or abolishing governance

A claim that governance is inherently virtuous or inherently oppressive

A moral judgment about people who favor or oppose rules

PART 4

The Human Mechanism

Living at the Horizon

Why Orientation Restores Proportion, Meaning, and Endurance

The horizon represents a stable orientation between immediacy and abstraction. It maintains proportion by limiting both fixation and escape. Living at the horizon sustains engagement without collapse into extremes. This chapter examines horizon orientation as an integrating condition rather than a prescription.

This mechanism applies where individuals or systems must balance local action with broader context. It governs sustained engagement across time without surrender to either immediacy or abstraction. It does not apply to moments requiring singular focus or total abstraction. Horizon orientation functions where ongoing proportionality is required.

Horizon orientation is often confused with moderation, compromise, or neutrality. Moderation averages positions. Compromise splits difference. Neutrality disengages. Horizon orientation maintains active alignment with both near and far constraints without collapsing them. The distinction lies in sustained orientation rather than positional adjustment. When horizon orientation collapses, systems tilt toward fixation or escape. Immediacy overwhelms context, or abstraction detaches from execution. Proportion degrades as attention narrows or floats. Endurance declines as oscillation replaces stability, and meaning fragments under pressure from unresolved extremes.

By this point, it should be clear that this book is not a warning siren. It is a map. Nothing here argues that civilization is doomed, that people are irredeemable, or that systems are beyond repair. It argues something quieter and more demanding: that survival is not automatic, and meaning is not delivered. They are maintained.

The horizon is not a destination you reach and then permanently remain within. It is something you return to every time you feel yourself being pulled toward panic or fantasy. It is a posture you repeatedly recover as the world pulls you toward escape, certainty, or resignation. It exists where attention is grounded and perspective is extended, where limits are acknowledged without collapse and possibility is held without fantasy. This is why the book began where it did: feet on the ground, eyes forward, not as decoration, not as slogan, but as orientation.

Living at the horizon does not require heroism. It does not require moral purity, brilliance, or consistency without failure. It requires presence. It requires the capacity to remain engaged without demanding guarantees and to act without mistaking effort for omnipotence. This posture is often misunderstood as resignation, but it is closer to maturity, a form of responsibility that remains steady without retreating from difficulty.

Endurance depends on proportion. Humans can sustain remarkable strain when effort remains oriented, when work is real, limits are visible, and responsibility connects to outcome. What breaks people is not difficulty, but diffusion: attention spread thin across abstract threats, moral demands without boundary, and conflicts that never close. What exhausts a person is often not the weight of one real burden, but the constant drag of too many undefined ones.

The horizon restores endurance by restoring edges. It narrows attention to what can be acted upon now while keeping context intact. It allows effort to convert into maintenance rather than vigilance and strain to resolve into repair rather than accumulation. In this posture, exhaustion becomes honest fatigue, the kind that follows work completed instead of the chronic depletion that comes from standing alert without end. The difference matters because one kind of tiredness can recover, while the other slowly hollows out judgment.

A horizon-oriented life is scaled correctly. It recognizes that the individual is neither all-powerful nor negligible. Agency exists within constraint. Responsibility exists without total control. Meaning arises not from total outcomes, but from sustained participation in systems larger than oneself.

The modern world often searches for meaning in resolution: final victories, total explanations, and complete justice. When those do not arrive, despair follows. The horizon posture bypasses this trap because it does not wait for culmination. It locates meaning in continuity, where effort accumulates and responsibility remains connected to participation. Meaning, in this sense, is not the reward at the end of the process. It is found in remaining properly oriented inside the process itself.

Civilization persists not because someone eventually solves it, but because enough people carry their portion without dropping it. This is why the language of salvation and collapse both fail to describe how systems endure. Salvation demands a redeemer, while collapse demands inevitability. The horizon rejects both and instead describes a world that continues because people remain oriented long enough to maintain it. Continuity is not glamorous, but it is how most real stability is produced.

You are not asked to save civilization. You are asked not to abandon it.

That obligation is lighter than despair makes it appear because it is ordinary. Most of what sustains societies is unremarkable: reading carefully, maintaining competence, using words precisely, repairing what breaks, containing conflict, and accepting responsibility that extends slightly beyond immediate self-interest. These actions do not announce themselves, but over time they accumulate into continuity. They seem small because they are repeated. They matter because they are repeated.

The horizon posture allows this accumulation to be seen clearly. It removes the drama that obscures proportion and restores clarity to ordinary effort. It shows that endurance is not a function of optimism or fear, but of coherence sustained through consistent participation.

Coherence allows difficulty to be absorbed without disintegration. It allows disagreement without rupture and imperfection without abandonment. It allows people to remain inside systems without being consumed by them or detached from responsibility.

This book does not ask for withdrawal from the world, nor does it demand hardening against it. It describes a stance within it, one that refuses illusion without rejecting participation. At the horizon, responsibility is accepted without inflation. Limits are acknowledged without surrender. Care is extended without claiming ownership of outcomes.

That combination is rare, but it is sufficient. If there is a quiet throughline running beneath every chapter, it is this: certainty is not required to live well. Orientation is required. Proportion is required. Restraint is required. Accountability is required.

The horizon provides these without spectacle. It does not promise comfort, but it supports coherence. Coherence allows people to endure strain without losing themselves, to contribute without erasing themselves, and to leave behind systems that still function for those who follow.

Feet on the ground. Eyes forward. That is how humans remain oriented, and that is how systems remain functional.

Chapter 16 Resolve

If you remember nothing else from this chapter, remember this:

Living at the horizon is a sustained orientation that maintains meaning and endurance through proportion, continuity, and coherence rather than certainty or resolution.

What This Chapter Is

An explanation of the horizon as a repeatable posture of orientation rather than a destination or outcome

A description of how meaning is maintained through continuity, participation, and coherence instead of final solutions

A boundary statement showing that individual agency operates within constraint, not total control or insignificance

An account of how ordinary, accumulated actions sustain systems over time when orientation is maintained

What This Chapter Is Not

A claim that civilization will be saved or inevitably collapse

An argument for resignation, passivity, or withdrawal from participation

A moral judgment about virtue, worthiness, or personal goodness

HUMAN OVERRIDE

The Gap Between Stimulus and Response

CIVILIZATION DOES NOT PERSIST merely because systems exist. It persists because individuals repeatedly interrupt impulses that would otherwise destabilize those systems. The capacity for that interruption is not automatic. It is not guaranteed by intelligence, education, identity, or affiliation. It is a specific human ability that must be exercised deliberately.

Human override is the uniquely human capacity to interrupt instinct, biological momentum, social pressure, ego, or personal advantage in order to remain aligned with dignity, obligation, and proportion. Instinct is fast and useful, but it is not scaled for modern life. It narrows attention, accelerates certainty, and favors short-term advantage under pressure. Override is the counter-mechanism: the ability to slow down, re-check orientation, and choose a response that remains accountable to consequence.

A tribe is necessary for cohesion and growth, but it naturally concentrates moral concern toward insiders. Without override, cohesion hardens into exclusion, and exclusion hardens into hostility toward outsiders. Override does not abolish tribe. It prevents tribes from becoming the boundary of what counts as human. A village is a sustained community, a mix of tribes and individuals continually restrained by override.

Many moral systems attempt to compress override into a simple, repeatable behavioral directive. One durable formulation operates by forcing two movements at once: decentering the self from ultimate authority and extending one's own standard of treatment outward to others. Structurally, this expands moral scope beyond immediate tribe and reduces ego-driven distortion. The value of the formulation lies not in its branding, but in its efficiency at scaling concern beyond instinct.

Override is the mechanism that allows horizon orientation to remain stable under pressure. It is what makes discipline possible without cruelty, humility possible without collapse, obligation possible without coercion, conflict containment possible without dehumanization, repair possible without romanticism, and governance possible without moral shortcuts. It is not instinct, emotion, or intensity. It is the introduction of a pause between stimulus and response when the natural trajectory of reaction would distort reality, damage relationship, or compromise integrity.

Every stimulus carries momentum. Fear pushes toward self-protection. Humiliation leans toward retaliation. Advantage invites exploitation. Group approval draws people toward conformity. These reactions feel natural because they are natural, and they follow the patterns of evolutionary wiring and social conditioning. Without interruption, they run their course and complete the arc of reaction.

Override is the refusal to let that arc complete unchecked. Override does not eliminate instinct, and it does not suppress emotion. It governs instinct so that reaction does not outrun judgment, and it orders emotion so that feeling does not dictate outcome. Pressure is not denied. Space is created within pressure so that response can be chosen rather than discharged.

This interruption operates at multiple levels, and when it fails at any one of them, the consequences accumulate over time. Failure does not usually appear as a single dramatic mistake. It appears as repeated small accelerations in reaction that gradually reduce the distance between stimulus and response.

The most basic form is biological override. Biological override occurs when immediate comfort or self-preservation yields to a longer standard of responsibility. It is often imagined in extreme forms, such as running toward danger or protecting another at cost to oneself, but it is more frequently expressed in ordinary moments. Remaining in a difficult conversation rather than escaping it. Admitting fault when defense would preserve ego. Telling the truth when deception would reduce consequence. Acting ethically when no one is observing. In each case, the body prefers ease, concealment, or avoidance, and override interrupts that preference by substituting alignment for comfort.

The second layer is social override. Human beings are deeply responsive to belonging because approval stabilizes while exclusion threatens. For this reason, group dynamics exert powerful gravitational force on behavior and language. Speech shifts to match consensus. Laughter joins cruelty to avoid isolation. Silence protects status. Social override interrupts that gravity by refusing participation in distortion even when such participation strengthens in-group bonds.

Social override does not require theatrical defiance or dramatic confrontation. It requires quiet resistance to exaggeration and restraint in moments of escalation. It refuses dehumanizing speech even when that speech is rewarded. It introduces proportion into conflict rather than amplifying it. Because much drift spreads through social reinforcement, the refusal to reinforce distortion becomes structurally significant.

The third layer is moral override. Moral override interrupts advantage and applies standards consistently when inconsistency would benefit the self. It returns what could be kept. It enforces rules even when those rules disadvantage one's own position. It refuses to exploit weakness even when exploitation would be rewarded. Without cost, morality reduces to preference, but override introduces cost, and cost clarifies seriousness.

Yet not all interruption constitutes integrity. There is also what might be called false override. False override feels righteous but expands ego rather than constraining it. It escalates language under the banner of courage. It defines identity through opposition. It enjoys condemnation more than correction. While it may present as resistance, it often intensifies polarization and dehumanization rather than reducing distortion.

True override reduces intensity and restores proportion. False override magnifies intensity and deepens division. The distinction matters because the language of restraint can itself be weaponized. When interruption serves ego rather than responsibility, it ceases to stabilize proportion and begins to accelerate drift.

Override rarely collapses in dramatic fashion. It erodes incrementally as fatigue reduces the capacity to pause and fear accelerates instinct beyond deliberation. Incentive structures reward expedience. Repeated minor compromises normalize distortion. Each unexamined reaction shortens the distance between stimulus and response until the gap gradually disappears.

When the pause disappears, reflex governs behavior. When reflex governs collectively, drift accelerates across systems and relationships. What once required deliberate judgment becomes automatic reaction, and automatic reaction rarely preserves proportion under pressure.

Override follows a discernible internal sequence that can be observed in real time. A stimulus presents itself, whether an insult, a threat, an advantage, or a fear. Instinct generates momentum toward reaction, and that momentum seeks completion. Override introduces a pause within that acceleration so that evaluation becomes possible.

Within the pause, several questions emerge naturally. What response is proportionate to the situation? What preserves dignity for all involved? What maintains alignment with the chosen standard of conduct? From that evaluation, a deliberate action is selected rather than discharged reflexively. The sequence is simple but not automatic: stimulus, momentum, interruption, reorientation, and action.

Most override is not heroic and rarely draws attention. It looks like not escalating when insulted. It looks like refusing exaggeration to win an argument. It looks like declining to humiliate someone weaker even when correct. It looks like accepting responsibility without coercion. These actions are small, but their repetition maintains orientation across time.

Civilizational endurance depends less on dramatic sacrifice than on sustained restraint in ordinary exchanges. Stability grows from repetition of proportionate responses rather than from isolated moments of heroism. The preservation of the gap between stimulus and response is therefore not a moral luxury. It is an operational requirement for maintaining shared systems.

The Role of Ego

Any discussion of interruption is incomplete without naming the force most likely to resist it. Ego is not merely vanity or arrogance. It is the internal structure that protects identity, status, narrative coherence, and self-concept. It seeks consistency in how the self is perceived and resists humiliation that threatens stability.

Under pressure, ego accelerates faster than deliberation. When insulted, ego seeks restoration of status. When certain, ego fuses identity with conclusion. When afraid, ego seeks control through simplification. When ashamed, ego seeks concealment or deflection. When powerful, ego seeks exception from rules applied to others.

Ego does not primarily seek truth. It seeks preservation of the self as currently understood. To preserve itself, ego may reinterpret events, inflate language, minimize fault, exaggerate threat, or assign motive without evidence. It may rename retaliation as courage and frame escalation as principle. In doing so, it shortens the pause that override attempts to preserve.

Ego can override override when identity feels exposed or threatened. The mind may deliberately collapse the gap in order to secure immediate relief from discomfort. Immediate reaction feels stabilizing because it restores control, but that control is temporary and often distortive. Over time, repeated collapse of the pause reduces freedom of thought without the individual recognizing the shift.

Override exists to keep ego from governing reaction without examination. Ego itself is not the enemy because it performs protective functions that support identity and continuity. However, when ego governs unexamined, distortion becomes predictable and proportion declines. The preservation of the gap is therefore also the restraint of ego under compression.

The broader implications are structural rather than purely personal. Without override, literacy becomes manipulation, competence becomes arrogance, governance becomes coercion, and conflict becomes dehumanization. Systems may remain intact in form, but their orientation shifts away from proportion and accountability.

With override, proportion stabilizes. Responsibility remains personal even within large systems. Institutional frameworks retain coherence because the individuals operating within them interrupt impulses that would otherwise distort those frameworks. Structure alone cannot preserve stability without disciplined participation by the people inside it.

Human override is therefore not an accessory virtue. It is the mechanism that prevents drift from becoming collapse. It preserves the gap in which deliberation can occur and maintains the conditions under which correction remains possible. It allows disagreement without annihilation and power without domination.

The persistence of shared reality depends upon that gap being preserved repeatedly by individuals who choose interruption over momentum. Without it, reaction becomes identity, identity becomes ideology, and ideology displaces proportion. With it, pressure does not automatically produce distortion, and tension does not automatically escalate into breakdown.

Override does not guarantee agreement, and it does not eliminate conflict or remove tension from human systems. It simply prevents those forces from escalating unchecked and preserves the capacity for correction when pressure rises. It is the capacity that allows restraint to remain viable under strain.

Override does not operate in abstraction or in quiet theoretical space. It is tested where pressure is immediate and reaction is fastest: when insult compresses time, when fear narrows vision, when power tempts distortion, and when certainty invites dehumanization. The interruption described here becomes most fragile precisely where it is most necessary.

Understanding override as a concept is not the same as maintaining it in practice. The body accelerates, the social field tightens, and emotion intensifies. Under those conditions, the pause must be preserved deliberately rather than assumed automatically. If override is the gap that preserves proportion, then the conditions that strain that gap must be recognized clearly.

The central question is therefore practical rather than theoretical. The issue is not whether interruption is possible. The issue is whether the pause remains intact under pressure and whether individuals sustain the discipline required to preserve it.

Chapter 17 Resolve

Human override is the deliberate preservation of a pause between stimulus and response, allowing dignity and proportion to govern instinct under pressure.

What This Chapter Is

A definition of human override as interruption of biological, social, and moral momentum.

A description of how override preserves proportion by preventing reflex from becoming identity.

An account of ego as the primary internal force that collapses the gap and accelerates distortion.

What This Chapter Is Not

A claim that instinct, emotion, or conflict can be eliminated.

A promise that override guarantees agreement or removes tension from human systems.

A celebration of intensity, certainty, or moral performance as proof of integrity.

Maintenance is Not a Hymn

Why Civilization Endures Through Structure, Not Faith

THIS BOOK DOES OFFER reassurance, but not the kind that depends on promise, miracle, or sentimental certainty. False reassurance tells you that everything will work out regardless of effort or discipline. It asks you to trust an outcome that has not yet been built. Durable reassurance shows how things endure and how that endurance is maintained across time. It asks you to understand a pattern that can be repeated rather than a promise that must simply be believed.

There is a difference between comfort and stability. A coin flip can feel hopeful because it preserves the possibility of success. A slogan can feel comforting because it simplifies complexity into a memorable phrase. A promise can feel stabilizing because it implies control over uncertainty. But hope without structure is not stability, and comfort without mechanism does not produce continuity. Stability emerges when behavior aligns with repeatable systems that still function under strain.

Civilization has not endured because outcomes were guaranteed or because history moved in a straight line toward improvement. It has endured because humans maintained proportion when pressure intensified, contained conflict before it expanded, repaired what broke before damage spread, and restrained impulses that could destroy shared systems. These actions were rarely dramatic, and they were often barely noticed. Endurance did not arrive as a miracle. It accumulated through the repeated practice of disciplined behavior over long periods of time.

Reassurance, therefore, does not come from imagining rescue or waiting for rescue to arrive. It comes from recognizing mechanisms that have worked repeatedly under different conditions. It comes from understanding how continuity is produced rather than assuming continuity will appear automatically. When people understand mechanisms, they gain the capacity to act inside uncertainty rather than retreat from it. They stop waiting for history to save them and begin participating in the conditions that make endurance possible.

The mechanisms that sustain civilization are not mystical, and they are not abstract ideals detached from daily behavior. They are practical patterns that can be observed in functioning systems across cultures and generations. They are human patterns repeated often enough to become infrastructure for shared life.

The mechanisms are human:

Literacy preserves shared reality by allowing knowledge to move across distance and time without distortion. It stabilizes communication so that facts can be verified, corrected, and transmitted beyond individual memory.

Governance restrains scale by establishing rules that coordinate large groups of people who cannot rely on personal familiarity or constant agreement. It creates boundaries that allow disagreement without collapse.

Obligation binds generations by connecting present action to future consequence. It ensures that systems built by one generation remain usable for the next.

Repair outpaces collapse by correcting small failures before they accumulate into structural weakness. It keeps systems functioning even when perfection is impossible.

Override interrupts instinct by inserting a pause between stimulus and response. It preserves dignity, proportion, and responsibility under pressure.

These mechanisms are not miracles. They are patterns repeated until they become reliable. They are not dependent on belief, and they do not require extraordinary people. They require consistent behavior sustained over time. Their power comes not from spectacle but from repetition.

Another distinction sits beneath this one, and it concerns the relationship between certainty and uncertainty. Honest uncertainty is intellectually stronger than false certainty because it remains open to correction. Humans naturally crave certainty because certainty reduces anxiety and provides emotional closure. It is psychologically stabilizing to believe that ultimate answers exist for every question about existence, suffering, justice, and meaning.

Traditions often offer answers to these questions in forms that feel complete and reassuring. These answers can provide comfort and continuity within communities. However, reassurance built on invented certainty does not become stronger simply because it is repeated or widely accepted. It remains belief rather than knowledge, and belief cannot substitute for mechanism when systems are under pressure. Repetition can normalize a claim, but it cannot turn an unsupported claim into structural reality.

Certainty grounded in faith can feel stable because it resolves uncertainty emotionally. Emotional resolution can reduce fear and create a sense of order. Yet emotional resolution is not the same as structural understanding. When certainty rests on faith alone, it replaces uncertainty rather than confronting it directly. The result is not true certainty but a managed form of doubt that has been given a reassuring name.

Accepting uncertainty honestly is harder because it requires discipline without guarantee. It demands engagement with reality even when outcomes remain unclear. Yet it is also more stable because it does not depend on defending conclusions that cannot be verified. It does not require narratives that collapse when tested. It allows reality to remain larger than our explanations while still permitting action inside the parts we can understand. That is a harder posture emotionally, but a stronger one structurally.

This posture does not eliminate hope, but it changes the source of hope. Hope shifts from expectation of rescue to confidence in maintenance. It shifts from belief in inevitability to trust in disciplined action. It becomes grounded in behavior rather than imagination. Hope becomes less theatrical and more durable.

The reassurance offered here is therefore practical rather than emotional. It does not promise that nothing will go wrong. It does not guarantee that justice will always prevail or that suffering will disappear. It does not claim that history moves toward perfection. Instead, it shows that endurance has always depended on maintenance and that maintenance remains available to human beings in every generation.

Maintenance is not glamorous work. It rarely produces celebration or recognition. It often feels repetitive, slow, and unremarkable. Yet maintenance is what allows systems to survive stress without collapsing. It is what keeps infrastructure functional, relationships stable, institutions coherent, and communities intact. Without maintenance, even the strongest structures deteriorate. With maintenance, imperfect systems remain usable.

You do not need a promise of perfection in order to participate in maintenance. You need orientation toward responsibility and proportion. You do not need certainty about the future in order to act responsibly in the present. You need discipline that connects effort to outcome and action to consequence. The requirement is not omniscience. It is steadiness.

Reassurance built on illusion dissolves under pressure because illusion cannot absorb strain. It fractures when reality contradicts expectation. Reassurance built on structure endures because structure distributes strain across systems designed to handle it. It allows correction without collapse and adaptation without panic.

That is the distinction running beneath this chapter. One form of reassurance depends on belief in outcomes. The other depends on understanding mechanisms. One asks for faith in inevitability. The other asks for participation in maintenance.

Civilization endures not because someone sings its praises or celebrates its ideals. It endures because enough people continue to perform the unremarkable work required to keep systems functioning. They read carefully. They speak accurately. They repair damage. They follow rules that preserve coordination. They restrain impulses that could destabilize shared life. They carry responsibility forward even when recognition is absent. Continuity survives through these ordinary acts long before it is ever defended in language.

Maintenance is therefore not a hymn of praise or a ritual of comfort. It is a discipline of continuity. It is the steady practice of preserving function in the face of uncertainty. It is the repeated choice to sustain systems rather than abandon them when strain increases.

That discipline is available to ordinary people in ordinary circumstances. It does not require heroic talent or extraordinary belief. It requires consistency, restraint, and attention to consequence. It requires the willingness to act responsibly even when outcomes remain uncertain.

Reassurance grounded in maintenance does not promise safety. It promises coherence. It does not eliminate risk. It reduces preventable failure. It does not guarantee success. It increases the probability of endurance.

Civilization persists when maintenance continues. Civilization weakens when maintenance stops. The pattern is consistent across time, culture, and circumstance. Structure sustains continuity where faith alone cannot.

That is the reassurance offered here: not that the future is secure, but that the tools required to preserve it remain within human reach.

Chapter 18 Resolve

If you remember nothing else from this chapter, remember this:

Endurance comes not from promises of certainty but from the human capacity to maintain, repair, and orient within uncertainty.

What This Chapter Is

A distinction between false reassurance based on promised outcomes and durable reassurance based on structural mechanisms.

An explanation that civilization endures through maintained patterns rather than guaranteed results.

An observation that honest uncertainty provides greater intellectual stability than invented certainty.

A framing of maintenance as the practical source of reassurance available to human systems.

What This Chapter Is Not

A dismissal of meaning, belief, or personal faith.

A claim that certainty is always impossible.

A demand that people abandon comfort or hope.

A promise that systems will never fail.

Ego Under Pressure

Where Override Is Most Likely to Fail

Override is easiest to affirm in abstraction, where reflection is calm and consequences feel distant. It is most difficult to maintain when pressure compresses time and emotion accelerates instinct. Under strain, the gap between stimulus and reaction narrows. The body speeds up. The mind simplifies. The social field tightens. What was previously a deliberate space for evaluation becomes crowded by urgency and saturated with emotion.

Pressure does not remove responsibility, but it distorts perception in predictable ways. It changes scale so that small threats appear large and temporary discomfort appears permanent. It magnifies risk while shrinking patience. It amplifies ego while reducing perspective. It shortens the distance between thought and action until reaction feels inevitable. This is why override matters most precisely when it feels least available, and why discipline must be strongest where instinct becomes loudest.

Under compression, people do not lose intelligence or morality. They lose time. They lose space. They lose proportion. The nervous system prioritizes survival over reflection, and survival logic favors speed rather than accuracy. Override exists to restore proportion inside that acceleration. It does not remove pressure. It preserves judgment while pressure remains present. The point is not to become emotionless under stress. The point is to keep stress from becoming your only interpreter of reality.

The Ego Under Compression

Ego is not vanity, arrogance, or selfishness alone. It is the internal structure that protects identity, status, and self-concept. It monitors how you are perceived by others. It resists humiliation and defends narrative coherence. It prefers to be right, to be respected, and to remain secure inside its own story. These impulses are not inherently destructive, but under pressure they can distort perception if left unexamined. Under strain, ego accelerates faster than reason because preservation of identity feels urgent. The mind begins organizing experience around protection rather than accuracy. Attention shifts toward threats to reputation or belonging. Language intensifies. Reaction becomes more important than understanding. The speed of response begins to substitute for the quality of judgment. In those moments, being seen as strong can start mattering more than actually being right.

- When insulted, ego seeks restoration of status.

- When certain, ego seeks confirmation of correctness.

- When afraid, ego seeks control through simplification.

- When ashamed, ego seeks concealment or deflection.

• When powerful, ego seeks exception from constraint.

Ego does not primarily seek truth. It seeks preservation.

To preserve itself, ego may distort memory, reinterpret events, inflate language, minimize fault, and invent motives in others. It may convince you that retaliation is justice, that exaggeration is clarity, or that humiliation is correction. It may even persuade you that surrendering your position to regain approval is strength. These distortions often feel reasonable in the moment because they relieve emotional pressure. Relief, however, is not the same thing as proportion.

Ego can even override override. When identity feels threatened, the mind may shorten the gap intentionally. Reaction is labeled as principle. Retaliation is renamed courage. Conformity is framed as wisdom. In doing so, the interruption that preserves proportion collapses, and reflex replaces reflection. The most subtle loss of freedom is not external coercion but internal capitulation to ego defense. A person can remain outwardly voluntary while becoming inwardly ruled by reflex.

Override therefore requires recognizing when ego has entered the frame and when identity protection has begun to shape perception. The task is not to eliminate ego, because ego performs protective functions that support stability. The task is to prevent ego from governing reaction without examination. Maintaining the gap between stimulus and response is, in part, the disciplined restraint of ego under compression.

What follows is not advice for calmness or emotional comfort. It is a diagnostic guide for distortion under pressure, a practical reference for moments when reaction feels unavoidable and proportion is most at risk. The numbered sections that follow are intended to function as quick access points, allowing a person to re-establish orientation when time is short and emotion is high. They are less about feeling better than about seeing more clearly before acting.

1. When You Are Insulted

Insult is a status event as much as a disagreement. It signals that your position, competence, or identity has been challenged in front of others or within your own mind. The heat of insult often arises less from the content of the criticism than from the exposure of vulnerability. The body registers insult quickly. Heat rises. Language sharpens. The mind begins constructing retaliation before analysis has occurred.

Insult compresses time and demands immediate response. It invites humiliation as repayment and encourages escalation as proof of strength. Without interruption, reaction accelerates and conflict expands beyond the original issue. Under insult, distortion appears in predictable ways. Offense is exaggerated. Tone becomes more important than content. The goal shifts from clarification to victory. Public response becomes a means of restoring status rather than resolving disagreement. These reactions feel justified because they promise relief from embarrassment. What they usually restore first is ego, not understanding.

Override under insult does not mean silence or submission. It means refusing reflexive escalation and restoring proportion before responding.

Immediate interruption questions:

- What exactly was said, stripped of tone and assumption?

- Is my response about clarity or about winning?

- Will escalation improve understanding or merely restore ego?

- Am I about to humiliate someone because I can?

What preserves proportion:

- Separate content from delivery.

- Lower intensity rather than matching it.

- Correct without contempt.

- Delay response if emotional heat is still rising.

If insult governs reaction, the attacker wins twice: once by provoking you and again by recruiting you into distortion.

2. When You Are Certain

Certainty feels stable and reassuring because it reduces ambiguity. It often feels moral because conviction can resemble integrity. Yet certainty compresses curiosity and narrows perception. When ego fuses identity with conclusion, disagreement begins to feel like threat rather than information. Under certainty, the mind stops searching for counter-evidence. Language expands beyond evidence. Opponents become caricatures. Complexity is reduced to slogans. Confidence gradually transforms into rigidity, and rigidity reduces the capacity to adapt. A mind that can no longer revise itself may still sound forceful, but it has already started hardening.

Distortion under certainty often appears as speaking in absolutes, dismissing nuance as weakness, interpreting disagreement as corruption, and expanding claims beyond available evidence. These behaviors create the illusion of strength while weakening intellectual discipline.

Override under certainty does not require abandoning conviction. It requires restoring intellectual humility and maintaining openness to correction.

Immediate interruption questions:

- What evidence would disconfirm my position?

- Am I overstating the scope of my claim?

- Have I reduced a complex issue to a slogan?

- Would I accept this reasoning if it harmed my side?

What preserves proportion:

- Distinguish confidence from infallibility.

- Speak within the limits of evidence.

- Allow for partial truth in opposition.

- Resist language inflation.

Certainty without override becomes ideology. Ideology under pressure becomes dehumanization.

3. When You Are Afraid

Fear accelerates survival logic. It magnifies threat and compresses time. Under fear, projection feels like prediction and hypothetical risk feels like immediate danger. The nervous system prepares for defense, and attention narrows toward perceived threat. Fear distorts scale by exaggerating worst-case scenarios and minimizing available options. It encourages extreme measures in the name of safety. It converts uncertainty into urgency and urgency into reaction. These distortions can feel protective even when they increase risk. Fear often feels persuasive precisely because it speaks in the language of prevention.

Under fear, people may catastrophize outcomes, accept extreme responses as reasonable, transfer anxiety into aggression, or surrender proportion for the illusion of control. These reactions often produce short-term relief while creating long-term damage.

Override under fear does not deny risk. It recalibrates scale and restores perspective.

Immediate interruption questions:

- What is actually happening right now, not hypothetically?

- What evidence supports the worst-case projection?

- Am I reacting to present fact or imagined escalation?

- Would this response appear proportionate outside this moment?

What preserves proportion:

- Separate immediate reality from anticipated scenario.

- Avoid permanent decisions in temporary panic.

- Refuse to convert fear into cruelty.

- Maintain standards even when anxious.

Fear unmanaged becomes justification for distortion. Fear governed becomes caution without collapse.

4. When You Have Power

Power reduces friction and removes resistance. It makes consequences asymmetrical and increases the ability to act without challenge. Under power, ego expands because constraint decreases. The temptation becomes subtle: exception-making feels efficient, humiliation feels justified, and enforcement begins to feel personal. Power magnifies ego because fewer barriers exist to limit behavior. The absence of resistance can create the illusion of correctness. Authority begins to substitute for judgment. Discipline becomes enforcement rather than responsibility. The danger is not only abuse. It is the quiet belief that ability itself authorizes whatever follows.

Under power, distortion often appears as entitlement. Standards are applied unevenly. Dissent is silenced because it is inconvenient. Resistance is interpreted as disloyalty. Correction becomes punishment. These patterns erode legitimacy even when authority remains intact.

Override under power is restraint when retaliation is available and humility when authority is secure.

Immediate interruption questions:

- Would I enforce this rule the same way if I had less power?

- Am I correcting behavior or asserting dominance?

- Does this action preserve dignity or merely assert control?

- Would this decision withstand public transparency?

What preserves proportion:

- Apply standards equally.

- Separate authority from ego.

- Correct privately when possible.

- Avoid humiliation as a tool.

Power without override becomes coercion. Power with override becomes governance.

5. When You Are Ashamed

Shame compresses identity and magnifies error. It makes a mistake feel like a permanent definition of the self. Under shame, ego equates failure with personal collapse, and the desire to escape discomfort becomes overwhelming. Two distortions commonly follow shame: withdrawal and deflection. Withdrawal avoids responsibility and delays repair. Deflection attacks the accuser and protects ego. Both responses interrupt correction and prolong damage.

Under shame, people may minimize responsibility, shift blame, perform exaggerated apologies, or collapse into self-condemnation. These reactions often appear moral while avoiding genuine repair. Shame can imitate conscience while still blocking accountability.

Override under shame requires separating action from identity and restoring proportion between mistake and self-worth.

Immediate interruption questions:

- What specifically did I do, without expanding it into who I am?

- What repair is proportionate to the harm?

- Am I defending ego or addressing responsibility?

- Would quiet correction be more honest than dramatic apology?

What preserves proportion:

- Name the error precisely.

- Repair without spectacle.

- Avoid self-condemnation as performance.

- Move forward without denial.

Shame governed produces growth. Shame ungoverned produces distortion.

6. When You Want to Dehumanize

Dehumanization simplifies complexity by reducing people to categories. It turns individuals into symbols and removes the felt need for empathy. Under pressure, dehumanization feels efficient because it eliminates ambiguity, sharpens hostility, and makes aggression easier to justify. What would otherwise require conscience or restraint begins to feel clean, obvious, and deserved.

Language shifts first. Individuals become abstractions. Motives are assigned without inquiry. Contempt replaces evaluation. The emotional distance created by dehumanization allows harm to feel justified because the person is no longer being encountered as a person. Once contempt becomes normal, restraint begins to look unnecessary, and cruelty can start presenting itself as clarity.

Distortion under dehumanization appears in recognizable forms: reducing a person to a single trait, assigning collective guilt, assuming malice as the default explanation, and taking satisfaction in the suffering of opponents. These patterns do more than intensify conflict. They erode the moral and perceptual restraints that make shared life possible in the first place.

Override at this fault line is civilizational because the preservation of dignity is one of the foundations of shared reality. Once people are no longer seen as persons, proportion collapses quickly. Judgment gives way to contempt, and contempt prepares the ground for justification.

Pressure narrows the gap. It accelerates instinct. It magnifies ego. It simplifies complexity. Under compression, override feels unnatural because reflex feels urgent and immediate. But urgency does not eliminate responsibility. It reveals whether interruption is still available.

The question under pressure is not whether emotion is present, because emotion will always be present. The question is whether the gap remains intact and whether judgment continues to guide action. If the gap holds, proportion remains possible. If the gap collapses, drift accelerates.

Override under pressure is not heroic. It is disciplined interruption maintained when instinct is loudest and time feels shortest. That discipline preserves freedom of thought and prevents reaction from becoming identity.

Immediate interruption questions:

- Am I describing a behavior or erasing a person?

- Would I tolerate this language if applied to me?

- Have I replaced analysis with contempt?

- Does this framing increase clarity or merely hostility?

What preserves proportion:

- Critique actions without denying personhood.

- Avoid collective guilt assignments.

- Maintain recognition of individual agency.

- Refuse language that strips dignity.

Once dehumanization is normalized, restraint collapses quickly. Override at this stage is not optional if shared systems are to remain stable.

Chapter 19 Resolve

Override matters most when pressure compresses time and ego accelerates reaction; maintaining the gap between stimulus and response preserves proportion and prevents distortion.

What This Chapter Is

An explanation of how pressure activates ego and compresses the space between stimulus and reaction.

A description of common conditions in which ego distorts judgment under strain.

A demonstration of how disciplined interruption preserves proportion during conflict, fear, certainty, power, shame, and dehumanization.

What This Chapter Is Not

A call for emotional suppression or detachment.

A claim that instinct or emotion can be eliminated.

A denial that pressure and conflict are unavoidable parts of human life.

PART 5

The Retun to Human Scale

The Collapse of Scale

Why Systems Fail When Growth Outpaces Governance

Language does more than label reality. It establishes the scale at which reality is perceived. Words do not simply describe events; they compress them, enlarge them, and assign proportion before careful examination begins. A single phrase can shrink a complex situation into a manageable category, or it can magnify a minor incident into something that feels vast and threatening. Once language expands beyond its proper scope, perception expands with it. What begins as imprecision in speech gradually becomes distortion in judgment, and distortion in judgment eventually becomes distortion in policy.

Scale is not an abstract concept. It is a governing principle that determines how systems interpret signals, allocate resources, and apply authority. When scale is accurate, response remains proportionate. When scale is distorted, response becomes excessive or insufficient. Both outcomes weaken stability. Excessive response wastes capacity and erodes legitimacy. Insufficient response allows risk to accumulate until correction becomes more difficult. Scale is not merely about size. It is about fit, about the relationship between what is happening and how strongly a system responds to it.

For most of human history, perception and scale were naturally aligned because experience was bounded by physical limits. Human beings evolved in environments where threats were visible and consequences were immediate. Danger appeared within reach of the senses. Information moved slowly, and distance imposed natural constraints on awareness. Communities were small enough that cause and effect could be observed directly. When something broke, the damage could be seen. When repair occurred, the improvement could be measured. Proportion remained anchored because feedback was immediate and local. Reality corrected exaggeration because people could compare the story to what stood in front of them.

These physical limits created an informal regulatory system for perception. Rare events remained rare because they were seldom encountered. Local conflicts remained local because communication did not carry them far. Rumor could travel, but repetition required time, and time provided opportunity for verification. In this environment, exaggeration was constrained by lived experience. People could compare narrative to observation, and observation usually corrected distortion. The distance between claim and correction was short enough that proportion could recover before distortion hardened.

Modern systems have removed these natural constraints. Technology collapses distance and compresses time. Events that occur across continents now appear instantly on handheld devices. Images circulate continuously, and repetition occurs without pause. A rare occurrence can be replayed thousands of times in a single day. A dramatic incident can dominate attention long enough to feel representative of an entire category of events. Under these conditions, exposure begins to substitute for measurement. This is one form of normalcy bias. People assume that because a system is still functioning, it is still sound. Warning signs are absorbed into routine. Distortion becomes familiar. Delay begins to feel reasonable precisely when correction is becoming more urgent. At the same time, repeated exposure to vivid anomalies can make the exceptional feel ordinary and the statistically rare feel constant.

This shift changes how the human mind interprets reality. Frequency becomes confused with visibility. Magnitude becomes confused with intensity. Probability becomes confused with vividness. The brain estimates risk based on what it sees repeatedly rather than on what occurs most often. When vivid signals dominate perception, proportion begins to drift. What is emotionally near begins to outrank what is structurally significant.

The collapse of scale does not require deception or malice. It requires amplification. Amplification increases emotional intensity without increasing statistical significance. When amplification becomes constant, emotional force begins to override quantitative understanding. People begin to react to presentation rather than to magnitude. Urgency expands beyond evidence. Fear grows beyond likelihood. Policy follows perception rather than measurement. None of this requires anyone to be lying. It only requires repetition outrunning reflection.

This distortion is psychological as well as informational. The human nervous system evolved to monitor immediate surroundings, not to process a continuous stream of global signals. When individuals receive uninterrupted input about distant events, the brain interprets those signals as present threats. The body prepares for action even when action is unnecessary. Over time, this condition produces a persistent sense of crisis. A person may be physically safe while remaining neurologically mobilized as though danger were at the door.

Persistent crisis has structural consequences. Attention narrows. Patience declines. Decision cycles shorten. Institutions feel pressure to respond quickly rather than carefully. Under sustained urgency, systems shift from deliberation to reaction. Reaction may feel decisive, but it often produces instability because it bypasses verification and proportion. Speed begins to masquerade as competence simply because hesitation now feels intolerable.

Language accelerates this shift when vocabulary expands beyond its original meaning. Words such as crisis, emergency, existential, violence, and threat carry significant weight. They signal danger and demand response. When these terms are used too broadly, their precision erodes. If every disagreement becomes harm and every setback becomes catastrophe, the distinctions that support judgment disappear. Without distinctions, governance cannot prioritize effectively. Once language loses hierarchy, decision-making usually loses it soon after.

Loss of precision in language produces loss of hierarchy in decision-making. Problems that differ in magnitude begin to appear equal. Minor issues compete with major risks for attention. Resources are distributed according to emotional intensity rather than strategic importance. Systems become overloaded because everything appears urgent. When everything is framed as intolerable, nothing can be ranked correctly.

Governance is particularly sensitive to this distortion because authority depends on proportional response. When perception inflates threat, institutions feel compelled to act dramatically. Action becomes symbolic rather than practical. Policy becomes reactive rather than strategic. The response may satisfy emotional demand in the short term, but it often creates long-term imbalance. Institutions then begin managing theater instead of managing risk.

Where Growth Outpaces Governance

The collapse of scale frequently emerges during periods of rapid expansion. Systems grow faster than their regulatory capacity. Complexity increases faster than oversight. Information moves faster than verification. Authority becomes stretched across distances that exceed its ability to maintain coherence. Growth is not inherently destabilizing. Growth becomes dangerous when coordination fails to keep pace with expansion. Without governance proportional to size, systems lose alignment between action and consequence. They continue operating, but they do so with weaker feedback, thinner accountability, and less reliable correction.

Common indicators that growth has outpaced governance include:

Decisions are made faster than outcomes can be evaluated.

Responsibility becomes diffuse and difficult to trace.

Communication channels multiply without clear authority.

Rules expand without consistent enforcement.

Exceptions become routine rather than rare.

When these conditions appear, scale begins to drift because feedback loops weaken. Leaders receive signals that are incomplete or delayed. Frontline actors operate without clear boundaries. Correction arrives too late to prevent escalation. By the time consequences become visible, the system is already compensating for errors it no longer clearly understands.

The Role of Narrative in Scale Distortion

Human beings orient themselves through story rather than through raw data. Narrative organizes experience into patterns that feel meaningful and memorable. It allows individuals to interpret events quickly and share information efficiently. Without narrative, knowledge would fragment into isolated facts with no guiding structure. Data alone can inform, but narrative is what allows people to move together.

Narrative is therefore necessary for coordination. It provides coherence, direction, and shared understanding. It allows communities to respond collectively rather than individually. Yet narrative simplifies reality by necessity. It selects certain details and omits others. It assigns roles, motives, and outcomes. This simplification creates clarity, but clarity can conceal complexity. Every story highlights something, and every highlight leaves something else in shadow.

Distortion begins when narrative resists correction. When new evidence contradicts the story, the mind may defend the story rather than revise it. Facts are reinterpreted to preserve coherence. Language shifts slightly to maintain alignment. Opponents are assigned motives that reinforce the narrative frame. Over time, the story becomes more important than the reality it describes. At that point, narrative no longer serves perception. Perception begins serving narrative.

At this stage, narrative merges with identity. A position is no longer an argument; it becomes a marker of belonging. Questioning the narrative feels like questioning the self. Correction becomes threatening because it destabilizes identity. The capacity to recalibrate scale diminishes because the emotional investment in the story outweighs the evidence against it. Once belonging depends on distortion, clarity begins to carry a social cost.

The Recursive Loop of Distortion

Distortion rarely appears suddenly. It develops through reinforcement. Each stage strengthens the next until the pattern becomes self-sustaining.

A simplified loop can be observed:

Inflated language reshapes narrative.

Inflated narrative reshapes perception.

Altered perception changes behavior.

Behavior reinforces the original language.

Institutional response confirms the narrative.

This cycle does not require conspiracy or coordinated manipulation. It requires repetition without examination. Once the loop stabilizes, correction becomes difficult because each component supports the others. The system begins to operate inside a distorted frame of reference. People then experience the distortion not as distortion, but as common sense.

Consequences of Scale Collapse

When scale collapses, systems lose their capacity to prioritize. Everything appears urgent. Nothing receives sufficient attention. Resources become misallocated. Trust declines because outcomes fail to match expectations.

Typical consequences include:

Overreaction to minor events.

Underreaction to structural risks.

Policy volatility driven by public emotion.

Institutional fatigue from constant crisis response.

Erosion of credibility due to inconsistent decisions.

These outcomes weaken governance not because leaders lack intelligence, but because perception lacks proportion. Decision-making becomes reactive rather than strategic. Stability erodes gradually until correction requires significant disruption. Systems rarely announce this drift clearly while it is happening. They simply become more erratic, more brittle, and less able to distinguish noise from signal.

Restoring Scale

Correcting scale requires disciplined recalibration rather than dramatic intervention. The goal is not to reduce awareness but to restore proportion between signal and response. This process depends on measurement, verification, and restraint. It also depends on refusing the emotional rewards of exaggeration.

Key practices that restore scale include:

Distinguishing frequency from intensity.

Separating magnitude from visibility.

Comparing anecdote to pattern.

Using precise language to describe risk.

Allowing time for verification before action.

Restoration of scale also requires flexibility in narrative. Stories must remain open to revision when evidence changes. Identity must remain separate from conclusion. Correction must be treated as adjustment rather than defeat. A system that cannot revise its descriptions will eventually lose the ability to respond accurately to reality.

When scale is restored, systems regain stability because response aligns with reality. Resources are directed toward genuine risk. Authority operates with legitimacy. Citizens regain confidence in governance because decisions appear measured rather than impulsive. Proportion does not eliminate conflict or uncertainty, but it prevents them from overwhelming judgment.

Why Systems Fail When Growth Outpaces Governance

Failure rarely occurs because growth itself is harmful. Failure occurs when expansion exceeds the capacity to maintain coordination, oversight, and proportion. Without governance scaled to match complexity, systems drift into imbalance.

The principle is structural:

Growth increases complexity.

Complexity requires coordination.

Coordination requires governance.

Governance requires proportion.

When any link in this sequence weakens, stability declines.

Systems endure when growth and governance remain synchronized. They fail when expansion outruns regulation and perception loses alignment with reality.

Chapter 20 Resolve

Perception loses proportion when language inflates scale and narrative hardens against correction; stability returns when words, stories, and judgments remain open to recalibration.

What This Chapter Is

An explanation of how language shapes the perceived scale of events.

A description of how amplification and repetition distort proportion.

An account of how narrative simplifies reality and can resist correction.

What This Chapter Is Not

A rejection of narrative as a human cognitive tool.

A denial that technology expands awareness.

A claim that language or storytelling should be eliminated.

THE ANTI-HUMAN HORIZON

Balance Requires Correction

CIVILIZATIONS DO NOT USUALLY collapse because people suddenly become reckless or immoral. They decline because systems drift and boundaries soften until behaviors that once felt temporary begin to feel normal. The change is gradual enough that most people do not recognize it while it is happening. Daily routines continue, institutions still function, and the outward appearance of stability remains intact. That familiarity creates a dangerous illusion. It suggests that nothing fundamental has changed, even as the underlying structure begins to weaken.

History shows that collapse rarely arrives as a single dramatic event. It emerges from accumulated decisions that seemed reasonable at the time. A policy is extended, an exception is granted, a shortcut is tolerated. Each step appears minor, and each adjustment feels justified by urgency or necessity. Over time, those adjustments reshape the culture of a system. Standards loosen, accountability becomes inconsistent, and the discipline required to maintain stability begins to fade. The result is not immediate failure, but a slow erosion of reliability.

One of the earliest signs of that erosion is a shift in how violence is understood. Force has always existed in human societies, and there are moments when it is required to protect life or defend order. Responsible systems treat those moments as serious and regrettable, recognizing that violence carries costs that extend far beyond the battlefield. Trouble begins when violence is framed not as a last resort, but as a moral achievement. When harm is described as righteous, necessary, or honorable, restraint becomes harder to sustain. Negotiation begins to look weak, compromise begins to feel suspicious, and peace begins to appear temporary rather than desirable. In that environment, conflict is no longer managed as a problem to solve. It becomes a principle to defend, and stability becomes increasingly fragile.

A similar shift occurs when certainty replaces curiosity. Healthy institutions rely on the ability to question assumptions and correct mistakes. That process can be uncomfortable, but it is essential to survival. Systems that permit criticism remain adaptable because they can identify problems before those problems grow beyond control. Systems that suppress criticism lose that advantage. When disagreement carries risk, fewer people speak honestly. When leaders assume their judgments cannot be wrong, small errors accumulate quietly until they become structural failures. Certainty offers the comfort of clarity, but without correction it becomes rigidity, and rigid systems break under pressure.

There is another condition that is harder to confront because it feels so unnatural to the instincts that built civilization in the first place. For most of human history, even enemies shared a basic assumption. They fought over land, resources, power, and revenge, but they still wanted to live. They wanted their families to survive. They wanted their communities to grow. They wanted prosperity, continuity, and a future. That shared instinct created boundaries. It made negotiation possible, even between rivals, because both sides understood that survival was the objective.

The danger emerges when a movement rejects that foundation entirely and begins to elevate death above life. When destruction becomes a goal rather than a consequence, the normal logic that governs conflict breaks down. A group that seeks survival can be deterred, negotiated with, or contained. A group that celebrates death cannot be managed under the same assumptions, because its incentives run in the opposite direction of civilization itself.

This is not merely a philosophical problem. It is a structural one. A society depends on the expectation that people value life and continuity. When an organized movement promotes self-destruction as honorable and mass destruction as acceptable, it defies the very logic that allows cities, markets, and institutions to exist. It undermines trust at the most fundamental level, because the shared interest in survival—the quiet agreement that holds civilization together—no longer applies.

That condition is rare, but when it appears, it is destabilizing in ways that ordinary conflict is not. It is tragic precisely because it forces responsible societies into decisions that feel harsh and uncomfortable. People who believe in balance, restraint, and progress naturally want solutions that are gradual and humane.

They want dialogue, reform, and compromise. Those instincts are signs of a healthy civilization. They are the habits that sustain peace in normal circumstances.

Unfortunately, there are moments when those same instincts become insufficient. When a system faces a force that openly rejects life as the highest value, delay can allow the damage to spread. In those situations, stability is restored not through endless negotiation, but through decisive correction. The purpose of that correction is not punishment or revenge. It is restoration. It is the return to conditions where life can continue and institutions can function.

Every system that operates at scale understands this principle. When a machine falls out of alignment, it does not fix itself by wishing for balance. It must be reset. When a bridge begins to fail, engineers do not debate the physics. They intervene. When a scale tips too far, it is not corrected by patience alone. It is corrected by force applied in the right direction, at the right moment, to restore equilibrium.

Civilizations operate under the same reality. Balance is not automatic once it has been lost. It must be repaired. That repair is often swift and deliberate, because prolonged instability carries greater costs than decisive action. The goal is always to return to stability as quickly as possible, not to prolong conflict or escalate destruction. A short and controlled intervention, though difficult, can prevent a longer and more devastating breakdown.

War introduces another predictable strain on stability. Conflict is sometimes unavoidable, but it is intended to be temporary. The purpose of war is to resolve a threat so that normal life can resume. Problems arise when conflict becomes permanent, when institutions grow dependent on tension to justify authority or maintain unity. In those circumstances, emergency measures become routine and extraordinary powers become ordinary tools of governance. Resources that should support infrastructure, education, and long-term development are redirected toward security and survival. Over time, the system reorganizes itself around conflict rather than stability.

Language often reveals the progression of instability long before collapse becomes visible. The words people use shape the limits of what they consider acceptable. When groups begin to describe others as less than human, the moral boundary that protects ordinary life weakens. The change does not happen overnight. It begins with hardened labels and simplified narratives, then evolves into justifications for exclusion or harm. Once empathy is removed from language, restraint becomes harder to maintain, and the risk of violence increases.

Information plays a similarly critical role. Reliable knowledge allows societies to make decisions that reflect reality rather than assumption. When information is distorted, withheld, or replaced with convenient narratives, decision-making becomes unreliable. Leaders begin solving problems that do not exist while ignoring those that do. Citizens lose confidence in institutions that appear disconnected from facts. A system can withstand difficult truths because they allow correction. It cannot withstand false ones, because falsehoods prevent problems from being recognized until the damage is already severe.

Identity can also become a source of instability when it is used as a weapon rather than a bond. Communities depend on shared culture and mutual loyalty, but those bonds must remain compatible with fairness and competence. When identity determines authority instead of responsibility, institutions lose their ability to function effectively. Decisions become guided by allegiance rather than evidence, and trust erodes across the lines that connect society. Over time, factions replace cooperation, and the collective capacity to solve problems diminishes.

None of these conditions develop suddenly. They grow gradually, often in response to genuine pressure and real fear. Leaders make difficult choices, citizens accept temporary compromises, and systems adjust to new demands. The danger lies not in any single decision, but in the accumulation of many decisions that slowly reshape expectations. What once felt unusual becomes routine, and what once seemed unacceptable becomes tolerated.

That normalization marks the turning point where stability begins to give way to fragility. Civilizations endure when they maintain discipline, protect life, preserve truth, and accept correction. They weaken when those habits are neglected or treated as optional. The Human Horizon depends on steady maintenance rather than heroic intervention. It requires people who recognize that stability is not automatic and that balance must be actively preserved.

It is also important to acknowledge the emotional tension that accompanies these moments. People who believe in progress, fairness, and cooperation may feel conflicted when decisive action becomes necessary. It can seem to contradict the very values that define a healthy society. That discomfort is real, and it should not be ignored. The willingness to hesitate before using force is evidence of moral awareness, not weakness.

Yet the lesson of history is clear. Balance is not preserved by avoiding difficult corrections. It is preserved by making them responsibly and without delay. When a system falls out of alignment, repair must follow. When a threat destabilizes the foundation of civilization, restoration must be decisive enough to restore equilibrium and limited enough to prevent unnecessary harm. That balance—firm action guided by restraint—is the discipline that keeps societies functioning.

The Human Horizon is not sustained by perfection. It is sustained by maintenance, proportion, and correction. When those habits remain strong, societies recover from shocks and continue to grow. When they weaken, the horizon begins to recede.

It does not disappear in a single moment. It moves gradually, step by step, as the structures that support life lose their alignment. The responsibility of every generation is to notice that drift early and to act with clarity before the distance becomes too great to close.

Chapter 21 Resolve

Civilization loses balance when the shared instinct to preserve life is replaced by systems that reward destruction or resist correction; stability returns when societies act decisively to restore alignment and reestablish the conditions that allow life, trust, and continuity to endure.

What This Chapter Is

A description of the conditions that push societies out of alignment and make collapse more likely.

An explanation of why movements that elevate death above survival break the basic logic that allows civilizations to function.

An account of why restoring balance sometimes requires swift, disciplined correction to prevent prolonged instability.

What This Chapter Is Not

A call for permanent conflict or aggressive expansion.

A rejection of restraint, diplomacy, or proportion in the use of force.

A claim that stability can be preserved without correction when systems fall dangerously out of balance.

Chapter Twenty-Two

SKEPTICISM VS CYNICISM

Why Doubt Can Clarify Reality or Destroy It

SKEPTICISM SERVES AN ESSENTIAL role in human judgment. It tests claims, asks for evidence, examines the methods by which conclusions are reached, and remains willing to update its position when better information appears. In this sense, skepticism is not a rejection of knowledge but a tool for refining it. It operates through inquiry rather than dismissal and preserves the possibility that truth can be approached through careful examination.

Cynicism, however, functions very differently. Where skepticism begins with a question, cynicism begins with a conclusion. It assumes corruption before examination and treats bad faith as the default explanation for nearly every action or claim. Information is not evaluated for its accuracy but interpreted primarily as a form of manipulation. Under this posture, new evidence rarely changes judgment because the expectation of deceit has already been established.

The distinction between these two orientations is subtle but important. Skepticism asks, What is true? Cynicism asks, Who is lying? The first question seeks understanding; the second assumes deception and searches only for confirmation. Legitimacy certainly matters, incentives certainly matter, and corruption does exist in many systems. Yet when legitimacy is denied universally, evidence ceases to function as evidence. Claims are no longer evaluated on their merits but sorted according to tribal alignment. What appears credible depends less on proof than on whether the claim supports the existing narrative.

Skepticism therefore preserves proportion because it remains open to correction. It allows claims to rise or fall according to evidence. Cynicism, by contrast, tends to fracture proportion. Once distrust becomes total, the ability to distinguish between credible and unreliable information weakens. All institutions appear equally corrupt, all expertise appears equally compromised, and every explanation becomes merely another strategy of control.

This is why skepticism remains compatible with shared reality while cynicism gradually undermines it. Skepticism slows judgment down. It asks what can be verified, what remains uncertain, and what would count as disconfirming evidence. Cynicism speeds judgment up by treating suspicion as proof. Once suspicion begins functioning as evidence, correction becomes difficult because the conclusion no longer depends on what is discovered. It depends on what was already assumed.

Corruption is real, and history offers many examples of institutions that have abused authority or failed their responsibilities. Acknowledging those failures is necessary for any healthy society. Yet corruption does not function in the contagious manner that cynicism often assumes. A corrupted department does not prove that every department is corrupted. A flawed study does not demonstrate that all research is fraudulent. A captured regulator does not mean that every regulator is captured. When such conclusions are drawn, a specific failure is inflated into a universal judgment.

That inflation matters because it destroys gradation. Once all failure becomes total failure, there is no meaningful difference between partial corruption and complete collapse, between a biased report and a fabricated one, between institutional weakness and institutional illegitimacy. The mind loses its ability to rank problems accurately. When that ranking collapses, proportion collapses with it. Everything becomes equally suspect, which means nothing can be judged with care.

These distortions arise through recognizable patterns. One common pattern might be called temporal freeze: a failure observed at one moment is treated as proof that the same failure persists indefinitely. Another pattern is asymmetrical scrutiny. In this case, mainstream claims are interrogated relentlessly while contrarian claims are accepted with unusual generosity, often because they reinforce existing distrust. Evidence that confirms suspicion is embraced quickly, while evidence that complicates suspicion is dismissed or ignored.

A third pattern is motive substitution. Instead of asking whether a claim is accurate, the cynical mind asks what hidden agenda produced it, then treats the suspected agenda as sufficient reason to reject the claim. Motives do matter, but motive analysis cannot replace reality testing. A selfish person may still tell the truth. A compromised institution may still report a real fact. Once motive replaces verification, inquiry gives way to narrative sorting.

The grounded observer approaches corruption differently. They do not deny its existence, but neither do they universalize it. Instead, they maintain the ability to discriminate between cases. They examine institutions individually rather than collapsing them into a single category. They recognize that systems may contain both integrity and failure simultaneously. In doing so, they preserve proportion, which remains the only safeguard against drift into totalizing distrust.

Grounded skepticism therefore requires a double discipline. It must resist naïveté without rewarding paranoia. It must remain alert to manipulation without making manipulation the only frame available for interpretation. It must allow that institutions can fail badly while also allowing that some people inside those institutions may still be competent, honest, and correct. This posture is harder to maintain because it preserves complexity rather than collapsing it.

Drift toward cynicism does not depend primarily on intelligence. Highly intelligent individuals can fall into it just as easily as anyone else. What matters more is temperament. Different psychological tendencies can lead people down similar paths toward disproportionate distrust.

One common road into drift begins with intellectual overconfidence. The individual may be perceptive, skeptical, and highly attentive to patterns of power or influence. They pride themselves on the ability to "see through" systems and believe that this awareness makes them immune to manipulation. Over time, however, their identity becomes fused with this posture of negation. Distrust itself becomes a marker of intelligence. Instead of testing claims evenly, they begin protecting their distrust as a position that must not be challenged.

This path is seductive because it feels like independence. It offers the pleasure of distance, the satisfaction of pattern recognition, and the status of appearing harder to fool than everyone else. But once distrust becomes identity, evidence no longer serves correction. It serves performance. The individual is no longer asking what is true. They are defending the self-image of being the one who cannot be deceived.

Another road emerges from a different temperament altogether. Some individuals are deeply oriented toward loyalty, belonging, and moral clarity. They seek coherence and stability within their social world. For them, certainty provides emotional and communal security. When narratives arise that promise simple explanations and clear moral divisions, they may accept them quickly because those narratives reinforce their sense of belonging.

In this case, cynicism may not feel like skepticism at all. It may feel like loyalty to the group that "knows what is really going on." Suspicion becomes a bonding mechanism. Distrust is shared communally and reinforced socially. The person is not necessarily drawn by the thrill of negation, but by the comfort of clarity and belonging. Yet the effect is similar. Doubt becomes selective, and evidence is filtered through identity before it is examined.

Despite their differences, both paths can lead to the same outcome. The intellectually cynical individual and the instinctively loyal individual may both arrive at absolutist conclusions. Each may become resistant to correction, and each may begin interpreting evidence through the lens of identity rather than through careful examination. Once proportion is lost in this way, shared reality begins to weaken.

The damage appears gradually. First, trust narrows. Then sources shrink. Then counterevidence begins to feel insulting rather than informative. At that point, conversation changes form. People no longer argue over interpretations of shared facts. They argue over which facts are allowed to count. When that happens widely enough, public reasoning becomes unstable because the standards for judgment no longer overlap.

When that weakening occurs, education, social class, and cultural background offer limited protection. The loss of proportion does not discriminate. It affects individuals across every category because it operates at the level of perception itself. When skepticism transforms into cynicism and distrust becomes universal, the common ground that allows societies to deliberate together begins to erode.

This erosion has institutional consequences as well as personal ones. Expertise becomes harder to evaluate because all expertise is treated as captured. Legitimate warnings are ignored because warning itself is interpreted as manipulation. Necessary correction slows because no mechanism of correction is trusted enough to function. In this environment, corruption becomes easier rather than harder to resist, because indiscriminate distrust weakens the very distinctions needed to identify where corruption actually exists.

That is one of cynicism's great ironies. It presents itself as a defense against deception, yet over time it lowers the quality of judgment. By flattening all claims into suspected manipulation, it removes the ability to tell the difference between honest error, structural bias, partial truth, and deliberate fraud. Once those differences are lost, reality becomes harder to navigate, not easier.

Maintaining skepticism while resisting cynicism therefore becomes a critical task. It allows corruption to be identified without allowing distrust to consume every institution. It preserves the possibility of correction without abandoning the search for truth. In a world increasingly shaped by amplified narratives and collapsing scale, preserving that balance may be one of the most important forms of intellectual maintenance available.

The task is not to become more trusting. The task is to become more discriminating. Skepticism asks for evidence and remains open to revision. Cynicism begins with suspicion and resists revision because suspicion has already become identity. One posture protects reality by testing claims. The other destroys reality by making testable claims irrelevant. The difference between them is not doubt itself. The difference is whether doubt remains answerable to evidence.

Chapter 21 Resolve

If you remember nothing else from this chapter, remember this: skepticism tests claims in search of truth, while cynicism assumes deception and erodes the ability to judge proportion.

What This Chapter Is

A distinction between skepticism as inquiry and cynicism as assumed distrust.

An explanation of how universalized suspicion undermines the evaluation of evidence.

A description of how different temperaments can drift toward the same form of disproportionate distrust.

What This Chapter Is Not

A denial that corruption exists in institutions.

An argument that authority or expertise should be accepted without scrutiny.

A claim that skepticism itself is dangerous.

Chapter Twenty-Three

Village, Not Tribe

Why Civilization Requires Reintegration

Civilizations do not usually fail because they make mistakes. Mistakes are constant in every system. Civilizations fail when they lose the capacity to reabsorb those mistakes once they become visible. The difference between collapse and continuity often lies not in the severity of the error, but in how the community behaves after the error has been exposed. Error is inevitable. Reintegration is optional. That choice determines stability.

A tribe survives through loyalty and punishment. A village survives through correction and reintegration. These are not simply cultural differences. They are structural differences in how groups maintain continuity. A tribe responds to error by identifying betrayal and demanding loyalty tests. A village responds by asking a different question entirely: how people who have disagreed, failed, or been wrong can continue living together after the conflict passes.

A tribe asks, Who betrayed us?

A village asks, How do we continue living together?

That distinction determines whether a society becomes trapped in cycles of revenge or whether it stabilizes after periods of error and conflict. It also determines whether disagreement leads to fracture or to adjustment. The question a society asks after failure reveals the kind of society it actually is. This difference appears every day in ordinary settings: families, workplaces, schools, churches, and neighborhoods. It is not confined to politics or history. It is visible whenever people must decide whether correction will lead to restoration or to permanent division.

What Tribal Behavior Feels Like

Tribal behavior often feels familiar because it resembles family loyalty. It creates a strong sense of belonging and emotional protection. Members defend each other instinctively. Outsiders are treated with suspicion. Internal disagreement is discouraged because it threatens unity. Loyalty becomes the primary virtue. That emotional structure can be comforting, but it carries risk. When loyalty replaces judgment, correction becomes difficult. Mistakes are defended instead of examined. Criticism is interpreted as betrayal rather than as information. Over time, the group becomes more concerned with protecting identity than with preserving function. What feels like solidarity gradually hardens into a refusal to learn. Tribal dynamics tend to follow predictable signals: Noise increases. Language becomes emotional rather than precise. Positions harden quickly. Loyalty tests replace evidence. Disagreement becomes personal. These signals do not appear suddenly. They accumulate gradually. The shift often begins with frustration or fear, then escalates through repetition. Once tribal behavior stabilizes, correction becomes threatening because correction implies disloyalty. The group begins treating cohesion as more important than truth.

What Village Behavior Feels Like

A functioning village feels different. It still values belonging, but belonging is tied to shared rules rather than to shared emotion. Disagreement is expected because people recognize that mistakes occur. Correction is treated as maintenance rather than as punishment. In a village, stability comes from process, not from loyalty. The key signals of village behavior include: Noise is separated from substance. Complaints are examined rather than amplified. Rules are applied consistently. Correction is allowed without humiliation. Participation continues after disagreement. A village does not eliminate conflict. It organizes conflict so that it can be resolved without permanent fracture. This structure allows communities to survive error without losing cohesion. It makes room for accountability without making exile the default answer.

The Problem of Public Error

In modern mass society, error is rarely private. Individuals take positions publicly, often in front of large audiences. They defend those positions with confidence, attach identity to outcomes, and invest pride in narratives that support their views. When those narratives collapse, through failure, exposure, or changing circumstances, the collapse does not remain confined to the argument itself. Something more volatile enters the system: humiliation. Humiliation is combustible because it converts disagreement into identity damage. Once dignity feels threatened, the goal shifts from correction to defense. The person who was wrong becomes focused on survival rather than on learning. The group that was correct becomes focused on dominance rather than on stability.

When the side that appears victorious responds with mockery, public shaming, or displays of superiority, the defeated side rarely dissolves or quietly disappears. Instead, it hardens. Mockery creates martyrs. Permanent banishment produces underground identities organized around grievance. Once humiliation enters the structure, people stop asking what is true and start asking how to protect themselves. A person who has been publicly humiliated rarely concludes, I was wrong. Far more often they conclude, They attacked me. What might have been a moment of correction becomes the beginning of escalation.

The Noise Problem — A Daily Pattern

One of the most common signs of tribal drift is the elevation of noise over analysis. The loudest voice begins to set the tone of the group. Emotion spreads faster than evidence. Urgency replaces reflection. In a tribe, the person with the most noise rallies the group toward an instinctive reaction. The crowd moves quickly. Questions feel disloyal. The result is often impulsive and poorly examined. Heat becomes a substitute for clarity. In a functioning village, the same behavior produces a different response. The loudest voice is not automatically followed. It is evaluated. The first step in a village response is simple: Separate the noise from the complaint.

This distinction is critical because most conflict contains both signal and distortion. The complaint may contain a legitimate issue, but the emotional delivery may exaggerate the threat. If the group reacts to the noise instead of the substance, proportion is lost. Once proportion is lost, the group begins rewarding intensity rather than accuracy. A functioning village therefore asks: What is the actual problem? What evidence supports the complaint? What part of the message is emotional amplification? What correction would address the issue without escalation?

After this evaluation, the group often asks the individual to reduce the emotional intensity of the message. If the person can separate emotion from substance, the situation stabilizes. If the person refuses and continues escalating, the behavior reveals a tribal instinct rather than a cooperative one. Refusal to lower the noise often tells you more than the original complaint. This pattern appears constantly in daily life. It occurs in family disagreements, workplace disputes, community meetings, and online conversations. The difference between stability and chaos often depends on whether the group responds to noise or to substance.

What the Wrong Side Must Do

Reentry into a functioning village requires maturity. Reintegration does not occur through branding, rhetorical spin, or clever reframing. When someone has been publicly wrong, especially dangerously wrong, the path back is narrow but visible.

First, the error must be acknowledged plainly. Attempts to soften responsibility through elaborate explanations or shifting blame prolong distrust rather than repair it.

Second, self-exonerating narratives must be avoided. Reintegration is not accomplished by explaining why the mistake was understandable or inevitable. It is accomplished by demonstrating that the behavior has changed.

Third, correction must occur without demanding applause. A society cannot function if every admission of error becomes a performance. Repentance staged for public approval is still too centered on the self.

Those who were wrong must also accept that reputational costs may follow the mistake. Accepting those consequences quietly demonstrates sincerity. Over time, the most persuasive evidence of change is not rhetoric but consistency. Trust returns through repetition, not through a single statement. The critical element is humility without theatrics. There is a profound difference between: I have already paid my price. and I was wrong. I regret it. I will not return to it. The first statement defends identity. The second restores trust. True reintegration is rarely dramatic. It depends on continuity rather than spectacle. It asks for steadiness, not image repair.

What the Right Side Must Not Do

Being correct can feel intoxicating. When a position proves accurate after conflict or uncertainty, the emotional reward can be powerful. Relief mixes with vindication. Confidence increases. The temptation to assert dominance becomes strong. Yet correctness is not a license for humiliation. If the side that was correct begins to treat correctness as authority, the village begins to fracture. Dominance replaces cooperation. Victory replaces stability. Being right about the error does not automatically make a person wise about what should happen next.

Three impulses tend to emerge in these moments: Endless mockery. Public humiliation rituals. Permanent suspicion.

Each impulse feels emotionally satisfying. Each impulse also destabilizes the system. Mockery may feel justified, but it rarely persuades. Humiliation may feel deserved, but it rarely corrects. Permanent suspicion ensures permanent division. A functioning village must resist these impulses even when anger feels legitimate. Otherwise the side that was correct begins reproducing the very tribal behavior it claims to oppose.

Why Humiliation Creates Martyrs

History repeatedly reveals the same pattern. When individuals are cornered socially, ridiculed publicly, and denied a path back into the community, they rarely accept correction quietly. Instead, they convert shame into identity.

The logic is simple: If reintegration is impossible, resistance becomes the only remaining option.

Once resistance becomes identity, correction becomes irrelevant. The person is no longer trying to be right. They are trying to survive. This transformation explains why humiliation often produces long-term instability. The immediate emotional reward of dominance creates future conflict. The short-term satisfaction of punishment becomes the seed of long-term division. Shame that has no exit does not disappear. It reorganizes itself into grievance. For this reason, the village must prevent the creation of martyrs, even when anger feels justified.

The Maturity Requirement

None of this is soft. None of it is permissive. Reintegration requires restraint from all sides. Those who were correct must suppress the instinct toward dominance. Those who were wrong must suppress the instinct toward defensiveness. Both must suppress the instinct toward revenge. Civilization depends on the deliberate restraint of instinct. The impulse toward eye-for-an-eye justice is ancient. It is deeply embedded in human psychology. Tribal systems rely on that impulse to enforce loyalty. Civilized systems restrain that impulse to preserve continuity. The difference is not whether anger exists. The difference is whether anger is allowed to govern the terms of continued life together. That restraint is the mark of adult civilization.

The Standard for Reentry

Functioning villages rely on a simple standard for reintegration: Correction. Consistency. Time.

If an individual acknowledges error, stops the behavior that caused the error, and demonstrates consistent alignment with shared norms over time, the village gradually restores trust. The past is remembered, but it does not become permanent identity. Reintegration does not erase memory. It prevents memory from becoming an endless sentence. Continuation matters more than humiliation. The alternative is endless purification. When societies attempt to cleanse themselves repeatedly by excluding those who have failed, the circle of suspicion expands. Over time, the purification process consumes the community itself. Loyalty tests multiply. Trust collapses. Stability disappears. A society can become so committed to moral sorting that it loses the ability to remain a society. Civilizations that pursue endless purification often collapse not because they are weak, but because they fragment under permanent division.

Historical Patterns of Reintegration

Societies have confronted this problem repeatedly, and the outcomes follow recognizable patterns. One pattern appears when punishment is imposed without any path toward reintegration. After large conflicts, defeated groups that were humiliated and excluded often formed underground movements organized around grievance. Without reintegration, correction became impossible. Defeat remained politically active because it was never socially absorbed.

Another pattern appears in movements that attempt total purification. Revolutions that begin by excluding former opponents often expand suspicion until members begin turning against each other. Loyalty tests intensify. Internal fractures multiply. The movement destabilizes itself. Once purification becomes the method, almost no one remains pure enough for long.

A third pattern appears in societies that stabilize after severe conflict. These societies typically combine three elements: Clear acknowledgment of wrongdoing. Limited but defined consequences. A structured path back into participation.

Reintegration in these cases does not erase memory. It preserves continuity. It allows a society to remember the breach without living forever inside it. The guiding principle is simple: We remember. We correct. We continue. That principle has preserved more civilizations than punishment alone.

Reintegration

Tribal instincts are powerful because they feel protective. Loyalty feels moral. Punishment feels decisive. Exile feels clean. Yet civilizations are not preserved by instinctive reactions. They are preserved by the capacity to override those instincts when they threaten shared life. At the individual level, reintegration depends on the same Human Override described earlier: restraint of impulse to protect dignity and preserve cooperation.

At the civic level, reintegration is the same act operating at larger scale. Those who were wrong must override defensiveness. Those who were right must override dominance. Both must override ego. Without that restraint, correction becomes escalation. Without that restraint, disagreement becomes identity warfare. Without that restraint, survival gives way to fragmentation. Reintegration is not softness. It is disciplined restraint practiced in service of continuity. A tribe protects pride. A village protects the future. The difference between those two priorities often determines whether a society fractures under the pressure of its own conflicts or endures long enough to correct them.

Chapter 22 Resolve

Civilizations endure not by avoiding error but by preserving the capacity to correct it without permanently fracturing the community.

What This Chapter Is

An explanation of how societies stabilize after public error through correction and reintegration.

A distinction between tribal punishment dynamics and village continuity dynamics.

A description of why humiliation and permanent exclusion tend to escalate conflict rather than resolve it.

What This Chapter Is Not

An argument that wrongdoing should be ignored or excused.

A denial that consequences and accountability are necessary.

A claim that reintegration erases memory of past actions.

Chapter Twenty-Four

FINAL ORIENTATION

How Humans Remain Aligned in an Unstable World

CIVILIZATION DOES NOT REMAIN stable because conditions are calm. It remains stable because orientation persists even when conditions are uncertain. Alignment is not a permanent achievement. It is a repeated act of attention, correction, and restraint. Systems drift naturally. Perception narrows under pressure. Emotion accelerates judgment. Without deliberate recalibration, even capable societies lose proportion over time. Orientation is therefore not a belief. It is a posture.

A person who remains oriented does not assume control over outcomes. They maintain contact with reality as it unfolds. They measure claims against evidence. They separate signal from noise. They act within limits rather than chasing certainty. This posture allows continuity even when stability is incomplete.

Instability is not an anomaly. It is the normal condition of complex systems. Economies shift. Institutions make errors. Technology accelerates change faster than governance can fully absorb. Social tension rises and falls in cycles. Under these conditions, alignment depends less on prediction and more on maintenance. Some thresholds matter because once crossed, recovery is slow. Institutions can be rebuilt. Skills can be retrained. Trust can be restored. But none of these return on command, and none return quickly after long neglect.

Maintenance is the quiet discipline that keeps systems usable. Maintenance depends on people who know how to do the work, and those people can become scarce. A society does not lose stability only when infrastructure breaks. It loses stability when competence disappears faster than it can be replaced. It is rarely celebrated because it prevents visible crisis rather than producing dramatic success. Yet maintenance is what preserves roads, courts, hospitals, markets, and families. It is what allows coordination to continue after disruption. When maintenance stops, collapse begins gradually and often invisibly. Throughout this book, several mechanisms have appeared repeatedly. They are not heroic solutions. They are stabilizing practices that protect continuity across generations.

Proportion prevents overreaction and underreaction. Restraint interrupts impulse before escalation. Correction restores function after error. Reintegration preserves cooperation after conflict. Continuity sustains shared systems through repetition. These mechanisms operate together. Remove one, and stability weakens. Remove several, and drift accelerates. Their strength lies in repetition rather than intensity.

Orientation in Daily Life

Alignment is not maintained through theory alone. It is maintained through ordinary decisions made under pressure. A parent who pauses before reacting to a child's mistake practices restraint. A manager who corrects an employee without humiliation practices reintegration. A citizen who verifies information before sharing it practices proportion. These actions appear small, yet they accumulate into social stability. Most people encounter instability not in dramatic crises but in routine friction. Misunderstandings occur. Plans fail. Emotions rise. In these moments, orientation depends on disciplined response rather than emotional reaction. The question is rarely whether tension exists. The question is whether proportion remains intact. The same pattern applies to institutions. Organizations remain functional when leaders measure problems carefully, apply standards consistently, and correct errors without spectacle. They fail when urgency replaces verification or when identity replaces judgment. Stability emerges from predictable behavior rather than from perfect outcomes.

Why Escape Is Tempting

Under sustained pressure, people often search for relief in absolutes. Absolutes promise clarity, certainty, and emotional closure. They simplify complexity into a single answer. They reduce anxiety by eliminating ambiguity. This relief can feel stabilizing in the short term. Yet absolutes rarely solve structural problems. They remove nuance and discourage correction. When decisions are driven by certainty rather than evidence, systems lose flexibility. Over time, rigidity replaces adaptation. What began as confidence becomes fragility. Escape can take many forms. Some withdraw from responsibility. Others demand total control. Still others seek simple explanations that remove uncertainty. Each response offers temporary comfort while weakening long-term stability. Orientation offers a different path. It accepts uncertainty while preserving responsibility. It acknowledges limits without abandoning effort. It replaces emotional relief with disciplined action.

Shared Systems Require Shared Reality

Coordination depends on agreement about basic facts. Without shared reality, cooperation becomes difficult because participants operate from incompatible assumptions. Communication breaks down. Trust declines. Decision-making slows. Eventually, institutions struggle to function. Shared reality does not require uniform opinion. Disagreement is natural in any society. What matters is the ability to test claims against evidence and revise conclusions when information changes. This process preserves legitimacy even when consensus is incomplete. Language plays a central role in maintaining shared reality. Precise language supports proportion. Inflated language creates confusion. When words expand beyond their meaning, perception expands beyond evidence. Over time, misalignment between language and reality produces instability. Maintaining alignment therefore requires discipline in speech as well as discipline in action. Clarity protects coordination. Precision protects trust.

Responsibility Without Total Control

One of the most persistent sources of frustration in complex systems is the gap between responsibility and control. Individuals are responsible for their actions, yet they cannot control every outcome. Weather changes. Markets fluctuate. Other people make unpredictable decisions. Systems fail despite careful planning. Accepting this limitation is essential for stability. Responsibility focuses on effort and correction rather than on perfect results. When people demand total control, disappointment becomes inevitable. When they accept partial control, persistence becomes possible. Responsibility therefore operates within boundaries. It asks individuals to maintain standards, repair damage, and continue participation even when success is uncertain. This posture protects continuity because it prevents paralysis in the face of unpredictability.

Alignment After Error

Every system makes mistakes. Error is unavoidable in environments that involve risk and complexity. What determines survival is not the absence of error but the speed and quality of correction. Alignment after error depends on three steps.

Recognition: the problem is identified clearly.
Correction: the behavior causing the problem is adjusted.
Continuation: participation resumes without permanent fracture.

These steps restore function without requiring perfection. They allow systems to learn without collapsing. Over time, repeated correction strengthens resilience because it improves judgment and builds trust. Failure to correct error produces a different outcome. Problems accumulate. Confidence declines. Conflict intensifies. Eventually, the system becomes unstable because unresolved mistakes overwhelm its capacity to adapt.

The Role of Restraint

Restraint is often misunderstood as weakness. In reality, restraint is a form of strength that prevents escalation. It creates space for evaluation before action. It allows emotion to settle so that judgment can operate. Restraint protects dignity as well as stability. When people respond impulsively, conflict expands quickly. When they pause, conflict becomes manageable. This pause is the foundation of cooperation because it preserves the possibility of dialogue. Civilization depends on restraint at every level. Individuals restrain anger. Institutions restrain authority. Communities restrain revenge. These acts prevent temporary conflict from becoming permanent division.

Continuity Across Generations

Civilization is not built in a single lifetime. It is transmitted across generations through shared practices. Roads are repaired. Laws are updated. Knowledge is taught. Traditions are adapted. Each generation inherits systems created by those who came before and modifies them for those who will follow. Continuity depends on stewardship rather than ownership. People maintain systems not because they created them but because others depend on them. This perspective encourages responsibility without requiring heroism. When stewardship declines, systems deteriorate. Maintenance is postponed. Standards weaken. Trust erodes. Eventually, the cost of repair becomes greater than the cost of preservation. Stability then requires significant disruption to restore function.

Staying Aligned in an Unstable World

Alignment does not eliminate instability. It allows people to function within it. The world will continue to change, and uncertainty will remain constant. What determines endurance is not the absence of disruption but the persistence of orientation.

Staying aligned requires repeated attention to a few practical habits:

- Observe reality before reacting.

- Measure problems before responding.

- Correct mistakes without humiliation.

- Maintain participation after conflict.

- Protect dignity even during disagreement.

These habits create stability because they reinforce cooperation. They allow systems to adapt without fracturing. Over time, they build trust that can withstand pressure.

The Meaning of the Human Horizon

The phrase human horizon describes the boundary within which people can act responsibly even without certainty. It acknowledges that the future cannot be controlled completely. It also affirms that action remains possible within limits.

Standing at this horizon requires steadiness rather than certainty. It requires patience rather than urgency. It requires commitment to shared systems rather than retreat into isolation. These qualities allow individuals and communities to remain functional while conditions remain uncertain.

Civilization persists not because problems disappear but because people continue to maintain the structures that hold society together. Alignment is therefore a discipline practiced daily rather than a goal achieved once.

Book Resolve

If you remember nothing else from this book, remember this:

Civilization persists when humans remain oriented to reality and maintain shared systems through proportion, restraint, and continuity rather than escape or absolutes.

Feet on the ground. Eyes forward. That is how humans stand. That is how systems endure. That is our human horizon.

What This Book Is

A descriptive account of how humans orient, escape, and re-orient within shared systems

An examination of the mechanisms that allow meaning, competence, and coordination to persist at scale

A clarification of how responsibility operates without total control or moral resolution

A framework for understanding endurance as maintenance rather than triumph

What This Book Is Not

A manifesto, warning, or declaration of moral urgency

A claim that individuals can save or are doomed to lose civilization

A justification for withdrawal, resignation, or coercive certainty.

If this framework is used to justify cruelty, exclusion, domination, or the erosion of another person's dignity, then it has been fundamentally misunderstood. The human horizon does not sanction tribalism. It does not legitimize hierarchy through contempt. It does not excuse the concentration of power through distortion.

The lens described in this book exists to preserve proportion, maintain shared reality, and protect the conditions that allow villages to function. When it is turned into a tool of division, it ceases to be a lens and becomes a weapon. That is not its purpose.

If you forget the structure, remember this:

Things hold together when people face what is real, do their part, and keep shared systems working instead of chasing fantasies or forcing absolutes.

This book is not about saving the world or declaring doom.
It is about staying steady.
Fixing what can be fixed.
Maintaining what must be maintained.
Refusing to use ideas as weapons against other people.

Feet on the ground.
Eyes forward.
That is how humans stand.
That is how systems endure.
That is our human horizon.

Chapter Twenty-Five

AFTERWORD

You don't owe the world certainty. You owe it and yourself, honesty.

Be careful with the truth. Be gentle with people.

And try, as long as you're here, to live at the horizon.

~ Lee Scott

Live long and prosper.

~ Spock

We're all called to be responsible neighbors.

~ Mister Rogers

The living have an obligation to the dead to keep trying. That's how humanity works.

~ Pas